# Beyond Patriotism

## From Truman to Obama

### James R. Flynn

**imprint-academic.com**

Published in the UK by
Imprint Academic, PO Box 200, Exeter EX5 5YX, UK
Published in the USA by
Imprint Academic, Philosophy Documentation Center
PO Box 7147, Charlottesville, VA 22906-7147, USA


ISBN 9781845403126


A CIP catalogue record for this book is available from the
British Library and US Library of Congress

*In memoriam*

## Joseph Henry Flynn

Tireless worker for reconciliation and peace

For your country, boy, and for that flag, never dream a dream but of serving her as she bids you . . . you belong to her as you belong to your own mother.

Edward Everett Hale. *The man without a country*, 1863


I know personally that Belgian women amused themselves by putting out the eyes of wounded German soldiers and forcing buttons ripped from their uniforms into the empty eye sockets.

Martin Buber, correspondence, 1914


We are not hurling our grenades against human beings.

Erich Marie Remarque, *All quiet on the Western front*, 1929


During the 1970s, the person most often proposed as the prophesized anti-Christ was Henry Kissinger.

History Channel, 2009


Partially driven by how much I love this country, I worked far too hard and things happened in my life that were not appropriate.

Newt Gingrich, Associated Press, 2011


Comfort me with apples for I am sick of love.

Song of Solomon 2:5


Totalitarian societies control information by suppressing what they consider inconvenient for their people to hear, while . . . democracies control information by swamping the truth in a deluge of disinformation which it is virtually a full-time job to sift.

Charles Shaar Murray, *The Observer*, 10 April, 2011


No state does right in the absence of goodness and wisdom

Aristotle, *Politics*, vii. 1323b 33-34

# Contents

## List of Maps

## List of Boxes

# Acknowledgments

Blackwood and Janet Paul are both deceased. I want their children to know how much a young scholar appreciated their encouragement when they published his first book forty-five years ago. *American politics: A radical view* (1967) contains material that updated, has become chapters 2 and 3 of this book. Pearson Education (New Jersey) has inherited the Paul list.

Chapter 8 contains significant excerpts from my book *Where Have All the Liberals Gone? Race, Class, and Ideals in America*. It is copyright © 2008 James. R. Flynn and reprinted with the permission of Cambridge. It originally appeared as a chapter entitled "The America who would be king" in David B. MacDonald, Robert G. Patman, and Betty Mason-Parker (eds.), *The ethics of foreign policy* (Aldershot: Ashgate, 2007). Once again, thanks to Ashgate for their permission. *Where have all the liberals gone* is mainly concerned with domestic politics and the American political tradition and is a companion volume to this book.

I owe Jeff Scott a great debt for bringing this book and Imprint Academic together. He is a man of wide knowledge and interests and has done much to help my work reach a broad public.

# INTRODUCTION

## Something New

# Chapter 1

# *The morally mature public*

I suspect that a morally mature public has evolved in America during the last 50 years. By that I mean that for millions of Americans the era of automatic patriotism is over, and they reserve the right to pass moral judgment on US policy, particularly decisions to fight wars on the soil of other nations. Indeed, I think we are approaching a tipping point at which these millions will think of themselves as citizens of the world first and US nationals second.

This evolution began in 1961 with debate about the morality of US participation in the Vietnamese civil war, and continues today fueled by debate about the wars in Iraq and Afghanistan. This book offers a moral compass to anyone, American or otherwise, who wants to think clearly about issues such as: whether patriotism or nationalism can be defended in the light of reason; if not, what kind of moral glue should bind a nation's people together; what policies they can in conscience support given a commitment to the common good of humanity; what they can do to make their presence known and influence their government and fellow citizens.

## A personal history

I was born in 1934 and therefore have a personal awareness of all of America's wars from World War II to the present. Moreover, my family has a strong sense of its own history that extends back to those who fought in the American Civil War of 1861 to 1865.

My knowledge of my ancestor's view of their obligations to America begins with the letters of my mother's grandfathers who fought for the Union. They lived in upstate New York near Lake Ontario, which was a stop on the underground railway, a clandestine route escaped slaves used to make their way to Canada. They were completely committed to the Union side, but their letters express no surprise that the residents of the South felt equally committed to fight for the Confederacy. The official history of Princeton University relates how the Northern and Southern students of the class of 1860-1861 held a party to farewell one another on the eve of their departure to fight and kill one another. They considered it perfectly natural that each had responded to the call of their native states. Robert E. Lee was offered command in both the Union and Confederate armies. He chose the latter because he was a Virginian even though he opposed Virginia's secession from the Union.

My father, one generation away from Ireland, always believed that English propaganda had duped America into entering World War I, tales of train loads of Belgian babies with their hands cut off. As a result, at the time of World War II, he only slowly came to believe in the existence of the Nazi extermination camps, assuming initially that it was just another English lie to bring America into the war. But he never questioned whether to obey when drafted for World War I, although the call came too late for service. My older brother never questioned whether to report in World War II. When North Korea attacked South Korea on 25 June 1950, I had just turned 16. The next day, my friends and I gathered at the Kalorama Road Park (in Washington DC) to discuss the news. While enthusiasm for actually risking one's life varied considerably, it never occurred to us not to serve if called.

A decade later, when American troops were in Vietnam, mainly from 1961 to 1972, whether one ought to fight "for one's country" became an issue debated by millions of Americans. I was 27 when the war began to escalate and became one of those who loathed what the US was doing. I decided that the slaughter was too great to be justified by any difference between the North and South Vietnamese regimes, and that my nation had debased itself by using weapons such as cluster bombs and Agent Orange. I do not know if I would have had the courage to go to jail rather than report for the draft, but was very pleased to be deferred as a student, father, and university teacher. Over the past 50 years, my conviction has hardened: I must be convinced on moral grounds that an American use of force is right before I acquiesce.

In addition, since the advent of the Nuclear Non-Proliferation Treaty in 1970, America has claimed the role of world sovereign, that is, it claims the right to license those who are "virtuous enough" to be allowed weapons of mass destruction, and to intervene militarily if a "wicked" nation attempts to get them. Ideas are catching. America's rhetoric about its global responsibility to pacify the realm immediately suggested an internationalist criterion that its policies must meet: whether they were serving or sabotaging bringing the world's violence under control. And that criterion immediately suggested that I owed my first allegiance to the peoples of the world rather than to the US government. The only thing that stood in the way of such a switch of allegiance was the concept of patriotism or nationalism and, as we shall see, I became convinced that nationalism was no more defensible that its close cousin racism.

## More than personal?

I believe that since 1960, millions of Americans have undergone the same transition from automatic patriotism to conscious rejection of that ideal in favor of an internationalist moral perspective. But this is subject to challenge.

First, one could argue that moral scrutiny of US wars is nothing new. Pacifists aside, controversy about America's wars is as old as the Republic. The Revolutionary War of 1776 alienated all those loyal to the English Crown and many of them fled to Canada so they could remain under English rule. Irish immigrants in New York rioted against the prospect of being drafted to fight on the Union side in the US Civil War, German Americans bitterly opposed US entry into World War I, and many Italian Americans opposed entry into World War II. However, these seem to me exceptions that prove the rule in that they are based on patriotic allegiances to nations other than America.

There were other critics whose allegiance was to some sort of internationalism. The Socialists opposed US entry into World War I as an imperialist war and Communists opposed the Korean War because of an allegiance to the Soviet Union based, at least in theory, on something other than Russian nationalism. Setting aside left wing ideology, there have always been enlightened individuals who judged America's wars as morally wrong, for example, William Graham Sumner and Elihu Root (who later received the Nobel Peace prize) opposed the Spanish-American War as nothing more than a war of empire.

Second, it could be argued that I make too much of Vietnam. Much of the opposition to that war arose out of special circumstances that have little to do with a new consciousness. Its duration of 11 years made it by far the longest US war up to that time, and the public was war-weary. It was a war that showed little prospect of victory, and even the US military began to have doubts on purely pragmatic grounds, such as the assassination of officers by demoralized troops.

Third, it could be argued that I am simply wrong that patriotism is on the ebb. After the attack on the Twin Towers on 11 September 2001, there was a rush of sentiment much like that of the pre-Vietnam era. Is not the real distinction one between defense of the realm and wars of empire? Historically, mercenaries or professional soldiers rather than a citizen army have fought for imperial ambitions. Perhaps US patriotism has remained constant, and the lack of universal commitment to Vietnam, and Iraq, and Afghanistan, is a phenomenon as old as Rome.

While acknowledging the grain of truth in all three objections I still believe that there is something new in America: a constituency of humanist internationalists whose numbers much exceed those of their predecessors and whose thinking owes little to traditional ideologies. But if I am mistaken, so be it. I have become an international humanist. Intellectual integrity demands that I justify my assessments of US policy and face the implications of my moral perspective. This is fundamentally a book of moral judgment and moral philosophy. I hope there are about 10 million Americans who want to think through the same problems. If there are only ten they matter to me. So read on and ask yourselves whether the shoe fits.

## America and killing

When one becomes aware that one's nation has done terrible things, it is easy to overreact rather like a youth who loses faith in an idol and is filled with hatred and self-loathing.

Two former officials, John Stockwell of the CIA (Central Intelligence Agency) and William Blum of the State Department, have detailed US interventions abroad since World War II (Stockwell, 1978; Blum, 1995, 2000, 2005). In passing, Stockwell shows that US intelligence furnishes whatever "evidence" it knows the President wants without regard to truth. I note this because of the foolish debate about "why" US intelligence found links between Saddam Hussein and Al Qaeda, and evidence of weapons of mass destruction, prior to the Iraq invasion.

These two men are bitter and this influences their judgment. They put 6 million deaths at America's door between 1946 and 1976, and their method of accounting would make the figure at least 8 million today. They use words like "holocaust", and those influenced by them say things like, if America had killed within her borders the millions she has killed outside her borders, she would rank with Stalin and Hitler as one of the great mass murderers of our time. I doubt anyone would have become critical of US policy unless it had done harm. But to compare America to the mass murders of history is first false and second, if true, would allow very little hope for a better America. You do not have to exaggerate the deaths US policy has caused to believe that she has gone astray. I make the total about 2,275,000 (add up the numbers in bold in what follows).

Stalin and Hitler killed by direct order. Stockwell and Blum credit America with every death perpetrated by anyone the US has aided in any way. For example, the US gave Indonesia the names of 5,000 Communist "operatives" at the time Indonesian was killing 500,000 of its Chinese citizens (they tended to vote Communist). This was not very nice. It is as if when Hitler was killing Jews, America made sure he did not miss Jewish communists. But it does not mean that you can credit the US with the whole 500,000. The fact that the US helped put Pinochet in power in Chile, and he subsequently tortured and killed 3,000 people, signals a higher level of guilt. The fact that the US created the Contras in Nicaragua, and continued to aid them while they slaughtered 12,000 rural people, justifies putting those deaths in the American column.

These "small scale" sins collectively would give a legitimate total of perhaps **30,000.** However, four cases swell the total.

First, imagine that Britain had sent troops to help the South in the later stages of the US Civil War, thereby prolonging the war by ten years during which there were an extra **1.5 million** killed, and left the country denuded and poisoned. This would be analogous to Vietnam. The bombing of Cambodia from 1969 to 1973, a part of the

Vietnam strategy, killed about **100,000**. Second, there are the deaths caused by a US initiative, those who died from 1990 to 2003 in Iraq (prior to the invasion) as a result of bombing and sanctions. The deaths from sanctions are a nightmare to estimate (see Chapter 5), but I put them at about **125,000**. Third, the Afghan war to date has killed about **20,000** and this in entirely an America creation, just as the previous war was a Soviet creation. Fourth, there is the Iraq war but its toll is more ambiguous. If an earthquake had removed Saddam and his henchmen, a civil war between Sunni and Shiite would have developed. No doubt, the US presence has made it more lethal—perhaps credit the US with **500,000** deaths or half of those killed to date? If the estimate of total deaths at one million seems high, see Chapter 5.

Americans do not see their nation as many others see it, huge, arrogant, unpredictable, an agent of death. When the hurricane struck New Orleans, American tourists in a Spanish town awoke to see a banner stretched over the square that said "Thank you Katrina." When I related this to an American friend, he said: "But that is disgusting, we give so much aid to famine stricken countries and other good causes." It was impossible for him to understand that the banner was not there out of pure malice. It was there because a force apparently omnipotent and mindless had been humbled by a force even more potent and mindless. It was there because Katrina had taught a nation so smug and secure, and so ready to inflict pain on others, how it feels to be vulnerable and weak.

### Morals and politics

The body count above is not meant to evidence some absurd thesis such as that the world would be better off without America. The American government has saved many lives through humanitarian aid and disaster relief. It has helped kill many by saturating the Middle East with arms. American citizens abroad have done many good works. American corporations are trying to get Africans addicted to tobacco. The American armed forces help to defeat Hitler and surely did much to intimidate Stalin. They have also done a lot of unnecessary killing. I am not judging America's soul but only its decisions to utilize force outside its own borders. These intervention have, I think, profoundly and rightly affected the psychology of its citizens.

Throughout most of my life, the nation potent enough to make history by using force was my nation of birth. Beginning at the age of 11, when Atomic bombs were dropped on Hiroshima and Nagasaki, I wanted to know just who made such decisions and what they were thinking. The A-bomb decision had as its backdrop the Cold War, that great rivalry between the United States and Russia that blighted the lives of all those in my generation by giving us world destruction as a constant companion. In 1945, Stalin and Truman were already at war in their minds even if the actual declaration of the Cold War was a year or two away. And when the Cold War ended, it became clear that the pacification of the world had become, if anything, more difficult. It was clear that if I wished to have any conceptual control over my time, I must form an opinion about certain questions.

Part I (Chapters 2 and 3) asks whether America "started" the Cold War (no), whether it was criminal to drop the Atomic Bomb (no), why have America and China been close to all-out war, and why did America sponsor the Cuban invasion. It will also analyze how America decides whether to use force outside its borders, knowledge we need if we want to alter policy. Part II (Chapters 4 to 6) explores the decisions that have alienated so many Americans from automatic patriotism. Why did America intervene in Vietnam and Iraq, and what kind of moral judgment should we pass on those interventions.

Part III (Chapters 7 to 9) addresses three questions. Why we should suppress any residual nationalism or patriotism we may feel in favor of becoming post-national people. What America should do if it really wants to play the role of world sovereign, and maximize the chances of the long-term survival and wellbeing of humanity. And finally, there is the political question. How can post-national people create, both in America and abroad, a moral constituency that might influence US policy?

# PART I

## The Patriotic Era

# Chapter 2

# *Two histories of the Cold War*

The Cold War was no one's fault but the inevitable outcome of two histories that fed off one another. These histories dictated the Cold War psychology which rested on these assumptions: the other side had unlimited ambitions and if it possessed a first-strike nuclear capacity, it would exploit its advantage fully; Communist and non-Communist were mutually exclusive categories and dictated a nation's allegiance; the world was a gigantic chessboard and any event anywhere that altered the status quo was one side's gain and the other side's loss. If either side had had the empathy to see history as the other did, the Cold War psychology would have been diluted, and the US vs. USSR rivalry would have meant less suffering by third parties and less danger. But even if the US and USSR had viewed each other through the spectacles of political realism, they would have seen two great powers competing for advantage. Moreover, one of these was so wicked that moral principle dictated that it not expand its dominion even in ways that the tradition of great power politics defined as "legitimate".

The Soviet and the American versions of the Cold War that follow are not official histories, which are exercises in political rhetoric, but what I think were the private beliefs of the more rational members of the two political elites. The first is based on conversations with American radicals that talked to (very brave) Soviet intellectuals in Russia. The second is based on a study of establishment historians or journalists, for example, John W. Spanier and Stewart Alsop. I do not think that either history makes any brute misstatement of fact, and will give sources for the historical claims they make. The interpretations put on facts are of course ones I would reject in most cases. The histories end with Khrushchev versus Kennedy because they are about the origin of the Cold War, that is, its first 20 years.

## The Soviet history

At least the USSR has never invaded the United States. America's determination to stamp out Communism, its refusal to accept co-existence, was signaled by its intervention in the fighting that followed the Russian revolution. America and its allies sent an expeditionary force into Northwestern Russia in August 1918 that fought on against Bolshevik troops until the spring of 1919, long after the German Armistice had been signed. Worse still, America, Britain, and Japan sent forces into Eastern Siberia to aid the counter-revolutionary forces led by Admiral Kolchak. These forces remained on Russian territory until spring 1920, eighteen months after the First World War had ended (Gabriel, 1948).

It was not until 1933, twelve years after the Bolsheviks had defeated their rivals, that America grudgingly granted recognition to the Soviet Government. During the 1930s, the aim of the West was to use Hitler to destroy the Soviet Union or at least to bring about a situation in which Hitler and the USSR would destroy one another. When Russia offered Britain and France an alliance against Germany in 1938, she was refused (Morgenthau, 1948). Rather, the West at Munich allowed Hitler to breach the Czechoslovak frontier, the only defensible frontier on Germany's Eastern border, so as to deflect the Nazis towards Russia. And then, when the USSR advanced into Poland to hold Hitler at a distance, and when she secured her Finnish border, the West accused her of aggression.

Had it not been for the refusal of Sweden to let British and French troops pass through her territory, the West would have come to the aid of Finland, an anti-Soviet state with strong Nazi ties. The West would have declared war on Russia and this despite the fact that France and Britain were already at war with Hitler (Neal, 1961). Even when Hitler threatened the West, the West looked upon Russia as an enemy rather than as a potential ally.

The Second World War made America, Britain, and Russia allies. Yet, the West still aimed at the destruction of both Germany and Russia. Its strategy was to make the USSR bear most of the cost of destroying Hitler so that when the War ended, the West would face a weak and helpless Russia and could dictate terms. America promised Stalin a second front in France which was deferred from 1942 to 1943 to 1944 (Spanier, 1962). Instead, she invaded Italy to protect British interests in the Mediterranean. America's Lend-Lease aid reached Britain when she needed it, but by the time it reached Russia in quantity, it was 1943 and the German armies had already been turned back on the entire Russian front from the Black Sea to the Arctic Ocean (Morgenthau, 1951).

America's strategy very nearly worked. By the end of the War, Russia had lost twenty million of her people. All of European Russia was in ruins: it was as if the United States east of the Mississippi had been leveled. And yet, America soon began to trumpet the preposterous charge that the USSR was about to attack Western Europe, and that she was a threat to America itself.

Russia had no navy, an inadequate air force, an army taken up with occupying Eastern Europe, a people threatened by serious shortages in a devastated country, and no atom bombs. America emerged from the War more prosperous than ever with an undamaged industrial plant that had expanded by over 50 per cent. She dominated the air and the seas and, along with Britain, controlled bases that encircled the Soviet Union. She had a monopoly of the atom bomb, the most powerful weapon on earth (Neal, 1961). The charge that Russia was poised for a program of unlimited expansion can only have been a conscious lie intended to provide an excuse for America's ambition, her ambition to establish herself as dominant in a sphere of influence that embraced the entire globe.

America's proof that the USSR was aggressive was that she did not hold elections along Western lines in the occupied countries of Eastern Europe, and that she deprived these countries of their freedom. Three of these countries about whose welfare the West is so concerned were allies of Hitler. Bulgaria allied herself with Germany even before the Second World War, and Hungary and Rumania declared war on Russia when Hitler invaded the USSR in 1941. When Russia was fighting for her life in the winter of 1942, Rumania and Hungary supplied 40 of the 160 divisions that Hitler commanded on the eastern front. And just which of these countries was democratic before the Second World War, which of them lost its "freedom" because of the Russian occupation? Certainly not Hungary with its Admiral Horthy, or Bulgaria with its monarchy, or Rumania with its Iron Guard, or Poland with its Pilsudski dictatorship.

The hypocrisy of the West in objecting to Russia's domination of her "satellites" is best revealed by pointing to Churchill's agreement with Stalin during the Second World War dividing Eastern Europe into spheres of influence. Russian influence was to be paramount in Bulgaria, Hungary, and Rumania, British influence in Greece, and Yugoslavia was to be autonomous (Morgenthau, 1951). It is true that the agreement did not extend to East Germany and Poland. We Russians can only say that Soviet domination there was not an aggressive measure but a defensive measure essential to Russia's security. Twice in twenty-five years Germany invaded and devastated Russia. The USSR cannot tolerate a united and armed Germany. The USSR can ill afford a weak and hostile, a pro-Western and anti-Soviet, Poland on its border to again serve as an avenue of invasion.

Imagine that the United States had been attacked twice through Mexico by a hostile power located in Central America and had beaten off the attacks at terrible cost. Would she then be willing to tolerate any Mexican Government save one allied to America? Would she then be willing to withdraw her troops from a portion of her enemy's territory if the remainder was allied with foreign powers traditionally hostile to America's very existence? The answer is obvious. America claims a sphere of influence, not merely over North America, but over the whole Western hemisphere. Her Monroe Doctrine forbids any great power to enter the Americas. When even small and helpless Latin American countries, such as Guatemala or Cuba, choose unfriendly Governments, the United States becomes hysterical.

The case of Greece is further evidence of Western hypocrisy. Communist units outnumbered non-Communist units during the Greek resistance against the Nazis in the Second World War. When the British dislodged the German army, Communists were in control of Athens and much of the countryside. The British drove them out of Athens by force of arms (Spanier, 1962). A year later, in 1946, rigged elections were held to institute a right-wing régime. The West showed great concern about the use of Russian troops and restricted elections to secure Communist governments in the satellites, but was quite willing to see similar tactics used in its own sphere of influence (Chamberlain and Snyder, 1948).

When the Greek Communists turned to guerilla warfare, Stalin stuck to his agreement with Churchill and gave them no aid despite the treatment they had received. All aid came from Tito's régime in Yugoslavia which, contrary to Western propaganda, was autonomous and pursued its own policy (Neal, 1961). The American President, Truman, lied to his people and claimed that Russia was supporting the Greek Communist military effort. He cited Greece as proof of Russian aggressiveness and announced the Truman Doctrine, that the United States would defend free nations everywhere from Communist subjugation.

The United States also expressed surprise and alarm at Russia's demands on Turkey for revision of the Montreux Convention and co-administration of the Dardanelles by all Black Sea powers. This was designed to break the Turkish monopoly of control over the Straits (a control Turkey had exercised to allow German warships into the Black Sea), and thus protect Russia from hostile warships and secure free passage for her own ships. America chose to ignore the fact that the USSR had been promised a revision of the Montreux Convention at Potsdam in 1945 (Chamberlain and Snyder, 1948).

This was not the only war-time promise that was broken. America had held out the hope that the USSR would receive economic aid after the War to help her rebuild her shattered country. The Russian request for a loan got "lost" at the State Department (Neal, 1961). Instead, Russia received the insult of the Marshall Plan. She was told that to qualify for aid she would have to abandon her own plans for reconstruction and submit to those of American capitalists. American journalists crowed over the cleverness of the United States in offering Russia aid that she could not accept, while adding that if by chance the USSR did respond, the American Congress would reject the whole program (Spanier, 1962).

The final item in the American indictment was the Czech "coup" of 1948. She chose to treat this event as if it were a matter of conquest by the Soviet Union, as if Russian troops had entered Czechoslovakia. In fact, the coup was perpetrated by the Czechs themselves. American troops as well as Russian troops were stationed in neighboring countries, and there was no evidence of popular unrest or protest within Czechoslovakia. The Czech Communist Party emerged as easily the largest party in the open election of

1946. If the West is puzzled by the strength of the Czech Communists and by the acquiescence of non-Communist Czechs in affiliation with the Soviet Union rather than the West, it should focus on its own behavior at Munich in 1938. The Czechs remembered how the West had betrayed them to Hitler. They knew that the Soviet Union would never waver in opposing the rise of a resurgent Germany (Neal, 1961).

America now embarked on a policy that was openly hostile. While propagating the myth of Russian aggressiveness, she began to multiply her arms, encircle the Soviet Union with bases whose planes carried atom bombs, and organize alliances for purposes of "containment". America even began to rearm Germany as an ally against the Soviet Union, Germany, the nation who above all wishes to destroy our country. Germany, who only ten years before had run amuck and even threatened to subdue the West. This stands as irrefutable evidence of the fanatic hatred that America bears for Russia and of the lengths to which she will go to satisfy her ambitions.

It was not so much that Russia feared Germany. By 1951, Soviet strength was much greater than it had been in 1941. It was what America's rearmament of Germany told us about America that Russia feared. It was clear that US policy aimed at nothing less than frightening the USSR out of her defensive sphere in Eastern Europe so as to establish hostile governments there. This was called liberation of the satellites. The ultimate objective was to put the Soviet Union at the mercy of the West and force her to acquiesce in whatever demand America chose to make.

America's policy dictated, of course, that the US monopoly of nuclear weapons be frozen into a permanent advantage over the Soviet Union. This raises the question of America's record in disarmament negotiations. The first US proposal came in June 1946 and was called the Baruch Plan. America offered to give up her stockpile of atom bombs but only after an extensive inspection and control system had been put into effect. This meant that Russia was to liquidate her own atom bomb project, already well underway, admit Western inspectors into her territory on a mission that would automatically enable them to pin-point military targets, and then trust the United States to dispose of her nuclear weapons. In other words, Russia was to disarm unilaterally and trust America to keep her word without any guarantee that she would do so.

Actually, America might well have kept her word because she did not promise to destroy her bombs but only to turn them over to the UN Atomic Energy Commission to be used for enforcement purposes against any nation found to be developing nuclear weapons (Barnet, 1960). Since the US had an overwhelming majority in the UN at that time, this meant effectively that the US would retain its nuclear stockpile intact at one remove. Russia would promise to perpetuate this American monopoly, submit to inspection, wonder when bombs were to be used against her because of a "violation" on her part, and pray for the day when the UN, which is to say the US, would decide that the inspection system was perfect and that the bombs could be eliminated.

All American disarmament proposals were calculated to be unacceptable. They gave the US the immediate ability to pinpoint potential targets in the USSR, which was to be followed by a long series of limited disarmament steps that would leave Soviet nuclear striking power at a disadvantage for the foreseeable future.

The best proof of American insincerity came in 1955. Premier Khrushchev accepted the whole range of US disarmament proposals including inspection, indeed, inspectors were to have the "right of unlimited access at all times to all objects of control". America responded by declaring all of her proposals up to that time obsolete. She suddenly began to argue that no system of inspection could be foolproof and that therefore disarmament was impossible.

---

### Box 1: First-strike capacity

What was a first-strike capacity? A great advantage in planes and missiles over your opponent makes possible the following sequence of events:

(1) You hit, not your opponent's cities, but his air bases and missile sites leaving him with only a few planes and missiles intact. You still have a large number of missiles and planes left;

(2) Your opponent cannot use his few remaining missiles and planes against your cities because you could then literally wipe *all* his cities off the face of the earth;

(3) He might hit a few of your bases, but then you could pin-point his last bases and destroy them, leaving him defenseless;

(4) At this point, you have "won" and suffered only "acceptable" losses (from fallout, etc.), that is, thirty million dead give or take a few million.

---

President Eisenhower proposed the open skies plan, that is, a plan whereby the location of all bases within both the US and the USSR would be made public (Barnett, 1960). As usual, this proposal demanded a major concession on Russia's part and offered nothing in return. The US sites were already public because the US had a great numerical advantage in bases and had no fear that a Soviet attack would wipe out her striking power. Because of the relatively small number of Soviet sites, secrecy was important, for otherwise the US would have a first-strike capacity to destroy all Soviet bases and eliminate her ability to retaliate (see Box 1).

US disarmament proposals could not be taken seriously as long as America continued to evidence her unwillingness to co-exist with Communist nations. America's China policy as formulated by Eisenhower and Dulles was a case in point. The Chinese Communists came to power largely through their own efforts by leading a revolutionary war against Chiang Kai-shek (Spanier, 1962; Neal, 1961). Despite this, America refused to recognize the Chinese Government, protected Chiang on Formosa, and assisted him in air attacks and guerilla raids on the mainland (Donovan, 1956). The US defended this policy on the grounds that China was an outlaw nation.

The Korean War was taken as proof that both Russia and China were aggressive, although Russia sent no troops at all and China committed troops only after a hostile American army approached her border. As for North Korea herself, it is worth noting that the North Koreans took up arms to unify their country only after repeated military provocation, indeed, far more provocations than led the North to subdue the South in the American Civil War.

Despite his public statements, Kennedy also refused to accept co-existence. When the Castro Government chose to take Cuba into the Communist camp, America financed, trained, and led an invasion by Cuban exiles in an attempt to establish a counter-revolutionary régime.

Concerning disarmament, Kennedy's actions spoke louder than his words. He talked about a peace race while embarking on a new arms race. America began to mass produce Polaris submarines, bombers, and guided missiles in an effort to attain a first-strike capacity. His talk of "negotiation from strength" was seen for what it was, a desire to increase America's military advantage over Russia to the point at which he could dictate terms. Finally, when Kennedy introduced his aggressive arms program, he justified it by claiming that the Soviet Union was mass producing missiles in an effort to attain a first-strike advantage over the United States. As usual, a lie was used as a cover for US aggression.

---

**Box 2: General Graves and General Knox**

There is no doubt that Graves annoyed General Knox, the British commander, who was an old Tory. The US press quoted Knox as telling Graves:

"You're fast getting the reputation of being a friend of the poor, and you must understand that the poor are nothing but swine."

I should add that the Czech unit the allied forces were sent to aid was not simply "escaping the German army". The fought against the Red army so effectively that they captured a string of cities.

---

### The American history

Most Americans and their government have always been opposed to Communism. However, there is no truth to the allegation that the United States pursued a consistent policy bent on the destruction of the Soviet Union after its inception.

An American army under General Graves sent to Siberia in 1918. It had two objectives: preventing Japan from annexing Russian territory; and aiding a Czech unit that had escaped the Germany army and was crossing Siberia. The first objective, an extension of America's open door policy in the Far East, was in Russia's national interest. Japan sent 70,000 troops to Siberia, as compared to the token forces of Britain and America, and had obvious ambitions. The presence of the American force created a situation which forced the withdrawal of all allied forces, including the Japanese, when the US withdrew. As for aid to Kolchak in his struggle against the Bolsheviks, Graves had instructions to remain strictly neutral which he obeyed to the letter

(Gabriel, 1948). He thereby annoyed both the Japanese and the British (see Box 2).

During the 1930s, American policy was not dictated by a preference for Hitler over Communism. The isolationists had wide support and controlled the Senate. It was not so much a matter that Americans opposed an alliance against Hitler as that they were against alliances or "foreign entanglements" of any sort. As for the appeasement of Hitler at Munich and the plans of Britain and France to come to the aid of the Finns, the US cannot be held responsible for the actions of other nations. There was some sympathy for Finland, partially because she alone repaid the American loan that she received during the First World War.

The United States sent Lend-Lease aid to Russia as soon as she could in the Second World War. American industry did not begin to convert to war production until shortly before Pearl Harbour, and it was early 1943 before she had war materials in any quantity to spare. It was Churchill, rather than the US military, who argued for the postponement of a second front and, more important, many felt that he was proved right by the disastrous experiment at Dieppe.

During the Second World War, rather than hoping for the destruction of the USSR, Americans hoped for friendly post-war relations. This was particularly true after the Yalta Conference in February 1945 at which agreement seemed to come so easily on a wide-range of issues: the United Nations, the occupation of Germany, the establishment of self-government in Eastern Europe, and military action against Japan. The US looked forward to a new era of peace and goodwill under the sway of the UN (Spanier, 1962).

These hopes were dashed by the Soviet Union at the close of the War, particularly by the policies pursued in Eastern Europe. Britain, not the US, agreed to the partition of Eastern Europe into spheres of influence. When Secretary of State Cordel Hull heard of the agreement, he registered a strong protest with Churchill (Morgenthau, 1951). However, America did not lack sympathy with Russian fears about the use of Eastern Europe as an invasion route into the USSR. She was willing to concede that Russia had a special stake in the future of Poland, Hungary, Rumania, and Bulgaria and that she should be the dominant influence in the area. What the United States was not willing to concede was that the USSR should completely dominate these countries, add their military strength to her own, and remain poised with overwhelming military force on the border of West Germany (Chamberlain and Snyder, 1948).

Unsatisfied with the consolidation of an empire over much of Eastern Europe, the Soviet Union attempted to undermine the independence of Iran. In defiance of the Tripartite Treaty of Alliance of 1942, unlike Britain and America, Russia did not withdraw her troops from Northern Iran at the end of the Second World War. Indeed, she increased her forces, sponsored a "revolt" in Northern Iran, and set up a puppet government in Azerbeijan. Britain and America had to threaten to defend Iran by force to gain a Soviet withdrawal and save Iran from becoming a Russian protectorate (Spanier, 1962).

Soviet demands on Turkey went far beyond a revision of the Montreux Convention, something to which she was entitled. She demanded not only co-administration of the Straits but also the right to maintain two military bases that would, in effect, have put the Straits entirely under Russian control. She also demanded that Turkey allow her to annex the border towns of Kars and Ardahan. Turkey rejected these demands and an American naval task force was sent into the Mediterranean to her defense (Spanier, 1962).

The Soviet Union tried to expand her empire in Eastern Europe. Communist guerillas in Greece may have received little Russian aid, but the aid they received from Tito, at that time an ally of the Soviet Union, was crucial to their success.

When Tito cut off his aid in 1948, the guerilla effort in Greece soon collapsed (Spanier, 1962).

The Communist Party was the largest party before the Czech coup in 1948, but 40 per cent of the vote is not 51 per cent, and the Communists seized power by force rather than winning a free election. Note what was implicit in the reasoning of the Soviet Union concerning the Czech coup. If it is legitimate for local Communists to seize power in a democratic country whenever they achieve significant success at the polls, what about Italy and France? In elections soon after the close of the Second World War, the Communists polled 33 per cent in Italy and 25 per cent in France. Were they next on the list of nations to experience a "people's revolt'? Russia hoped to see her armies occupy country after country until she controlled virtually the whole of Europe (Spanier, 1962).

The Marshall Plan was, in part, a response to the Soviet Union's ambitions. It aimed at alleviating the postwar poverty and industrial chaos that afflicted Europe so that other nations would not meet the fate of Czechoslovakia.

But it also had the purpose of building an integrated European economy. Western Europe, relatively poor in foodstuffs, would profit from the farm surpluses of the East, and Eastern Europe (including Russia) would develop its industrial raw materials, raise its standard of living, and provide a greater market for Western manufactured goods (Dean, 1948). The Soviet Union wished to isolate the economies of Eastern Europe from the West and exploit their inadequate industry to make good her own shortage of consumer goods. America can hardly be blamed when she asked that all countries who wished to benefit from the Marshall Plan be willing to cooperate in economic planning.

The formation of NATO (North Atlantic Treaty Organization) in 1949 and the later rearming of Germany within the framework of NATO were responses to Soviet ambitions. The Czech coup occurred in February 1948, and in June of that year, the Soviet Union blockaded West Berlin in an attempt to isolate it from the rest of West Germany.

The purpose of the Berlin blockade was to force America to withdraw from the city and dramatize the fact that the United States lacked the will to safeguard the security of Western Europe. Western Europe might then feel, as the Czechs did, that it was at the mercy of the Red Army and had no alternative but to submit to a Russian protectorate. The fears of Western Europe had already found expression in the Treaty of Dunkirk in 1947 and the Brussels Pact of March 1948, which included Britain, France, Holland, Belgium, and Luxembourg. In other words, the formation of NATO was not a matter of the United States prodding Western Europe to join her in a military alliance. It was that the Brussels Pact countries, and others, hoped that their alliance would attract American military support (Spanier, 1962).

After the attack of North Korea on South Korea in June 1950, NATO began to build up its armed forces. North Korea was under Soviet influence at the time, and could not have launched her attack without Soviet permission. It seemed that the Soviet Union was about to abandon demands and threats in favor of outright armed aggression. While Russia lacked nuclear weapons and a powerful air force in 1946, she had the former by 1949 and was on the verge of achieving the latter by 1950. This posed a dilemma for the NATO countries. Until 1950, NATO had depended on American nuclear weapons to deter a Russian attack on Western Europe. Now that Russia was acquiring a nuclear strike force of her own, an American nuclear attack would bring Russian retaliation and mutual destruction. Therefore, the danger of an attack by the Russian army had to be deterred by a NATO force using conventional weapons.

Thanks to the failure of Russia to demobilize after the Second World War, the conventional forces of the Soviet Union and her satellites were overwhelmingly powerful compared to the armies of Western Europe. The only possible source of manpower to match the strength of the Red Army was West Germany and in 1951, the US began to press for the inclusion of German troops in NATO. In order to make sure that German troops would only be used to safeguard the security of Western Europe, they were limited to conventional ground forces and placed under strict NATO control (Spanier, 1962).

The Korean War shocked the West into action because it was such a clear case of aggression and because, as was the case with Hitler, it was justified by a charge of aggression against the nation attacked. The Communist claim that America armed and directed South Korea in an attack on the North is at complete variance with the facts. The belligerent statements of Syngman Rhee, the President of South Korea, had rendered the United States uneasy about his intentions. She therefore pursued a policy of denying Rhee the capacity to wage offensive war, and withheld modern artillery and mechanized units from the South Korean army.

Rather than being poised for aggressive action against North Korea, the US was woefully unprepared at the outbreak of hostilities. She had almost no ground forces outside of her occupation garrisons, and her divisions in Japan, the only forces close enough to stem the North Korean advance, were at 60 per cent strength (Spanier, 1962). In all of the United States, America had only a little over one division and the raw recruits initially committed to the Korean War suffered heavy casualties. As to whether North or South Korea was the aggressor, the essential question is which side set its troops to marching in force. North Korea was clearly the aggressor despite the fact that provocations occurred on both sides preceding the North Korean attack.

So much for the accusation that America built up her arms, formed alliances, and encircled the Soviet Union with bases in order to put Russia at her mercy. These steps were responses to specific acts of Soviet aggression. The best evidence of America's lack of aggressive intent at the end of the Second World War was the speed of her demobilization program. America did emerge from the War with the atomic bomb and a powerful Navy, Army, and Air Force. But within ten months of the defeat of Germany, America reduced her Army in Europe to only 400,000 men, most of whom were new recruits serving as occupation forces. The Navy and Air Force suffered similar drastic cuts. American industry was immediately converted to peacetime production.

Most significant of all, the US made no attempt to build a stockpile of nuclear weapons. Indeed, no real steps were taken in this direction until late in 1947, two years after Nagasaki (Barnet, 1960). By this time, the Soviet Union had made her intentions clear by her actions in regard to Iran, Greece, and Turkey. No theory that America aimed at a nuclear monopoly to cow the USSR into submission can accommodate this fact.

The Baruch Plan was a sincere attempt to put nuclear weapons under international control and prevent a disastrous arms race. What other nation has ever offered to give up monopoly control of an all-powerful weapon, asking only that it never be developed by others (Barnet, 1960)? Rather than reacting constructively, the Soviet Union presented the Gromyko Plan, which called for the establishment of a system of inspection only after the United States had destroyed its stockpile of bombs. The Soviet Union had already begun her own bomb project. What she wanted was for the United States to unilaterally disarm and trust the Soviet Union to follow suit by dismantling her bomb project and agreeing to a workable system of inspection.

America's wisdom in rejecting such a proposal was made manifest when Gromyko spelled out the inspection he had in mind in June 1947. Inspection was to be of declared plants on a periodic, preannounced basis thereby maximizing the opportunity to conceal violations (Carey, 1962).

All efforts to negotiate disarmament were rendered fruitless by the absurdity of the Soviet position on inspection. Until 1955, during nine years of negotiations, Russia refused to concede the possibility that bombs might be treacherously concealed after a disarmament agreement, or that fissionable material which could be quickly converted to military use posed a similar problem (Barnet, 1960). Khrushchev's about face in 1955 did seem to mark the beginning of a sane attitude towards inspection, although it left the amount of inspection that Russia was ready to accept somewhat vague (Barnet, 1960).

It is questionable how serious Khrushchev was because he tied his plan to a demand for immediate liquidation of all America's foreign bases (Carey, 1962). This unilateral concession on America's part would have undermined her nuclear striking power. This demand was modified in 1957 (Barnet, 1960) but as of 1960, the USSR continued to take an unrealistic position on inspection. She agreed to a series of graduated steps towards disarmament and inspection at each stage of the weapons eliminated. But she did not agree to inspection of the weapons that remained, or the unrestricted inspection that would ensure that no new weapons were being produced (Druckman, 1962). In sum, she did not agree to an inspection that would determine whether or not her overall military strength had been reduced to the agreed levels.

Given her record, how could America have trusted the Soviet Union to disarm? Deception and veiled threats had characterized Soviet policy from the time of the Teheran agreements right up through her attempt to smuggle missiles into Cuba in 1962. It is one thing to accept an imperfect system of inspection when the attitude of the potential violator is ambiguous. It is another thing when you have reason to believe that the potential violator has a fixed intention to destroy you whenever he gets the chance. The United States had no alternative but to defend herself in the arms race.

## The two histories assessed

I have no doubt that Stalin, like most nationalists, saw a coherent pattern of foreign aggression to which he had to "react". A Russian did not have to be a Communist to think that America was the aggressor in the Cold War. Despite all its half-truths, the Russian version of history is more convincing than most of the patriotic histories nations concoct to cast themselves in the role of eternal victim. I suspect that Stalin pursued Russia's traditional national interest; and that Communist ideology was primarily an instrument of cultural imperialism, a weapon like pan-Slavism, that gave Russia sympathizers abroad and could prove useful as a pretext for intervention. However, no one can go back and read Stalin's mind. The best we can do is ask: if the Czars had still ruled Russia and Communist ideology were absent, how different would Soviet behavior have been at the end of the Second World War?

The Czars acquired and attempted to expand a sphere of influence in Northern Iran, attempted to gain control of the Straits that would allow Russian access to the Mediterranean, and sought to absorb as much of Poland as possible. After victory over Napoleon in 1815, the Czar put his hand on the map of Poland and said "C'est à moi". It took the opposition of all the other great powers to force him to give way (Morgenthau, 1951). Czarist Russia aspired to a sphere of influence over Korea. This was the principal thing at stake in the Russo-Japanese War of 1905.

None of these objectives shows that Czarist Russia was particularly aggressive. In the game of power politics, it was traditional for a great power to seek control over a sphere of influence around its border, a sphere to serve as a buffer zone against other great powers. The Czars wanted to deny Korea to Japan because the Japanese were using it as a base for expansion on Russia's border. They wanted Iran as a buffer against British influence in India and the Persian Gulf. They wanted to control the Straits so that they could keep Russia from being attacked on her Black Sea coast as she was in the Crimean War.

Greece and Czechoslovakia lie beyond the traditional goals of Russian policy. If Russian troops had invaded and conquered these countries after the Second World War, it would have been alarming. That is not what occurred. The Soviet version of events is closer to the truth than that of the West.

No doubt President Truman honestly believed that Stalin was maintaining the Communist guerillas in Greece. But many historians hold that the aid did in fact come from Tito and, as Tito's break with Stalin in 1948 showed, Yugoslavia was never merely a Russian puppet. Stalin may have kept his promise to leave Greece alone. The Czech coup was tragic because this country had a real democratic tradition. The USSR encouraged the Czech Communists, helped them organize during the last days of the War, and was happy to see the nation go Communist. But it is also true that the Czech Communists managed the coup themselves, and that most Czechs acquiesced without resistance. This last probably was to a large extent part of the legacy of the betrayal of Czechoslovakia by the West at Munich.

After World War II, any Russian govenment would have wanted Russian troops as close to Berlin and German troops as far from Moscow as possible. No Russian government would have relaxed its hold on East Germany. In 1918, after defending herself against Germany, France occupied the Ruhr and the Rhineland. If she had been able to permanently detach them under a government subject to her influence, she would have done so. France has been bitterly criticized for relinquishing them when a resurgent Germany demanded their return.

This brings us to the central question: did the Soviet Union plan to march her armies West and conquer Europe? The conventional answer is that of course she did, but was deterred by America's nuclear power. Actually, the answer is not so obvious. Much is made of the large army that the

Soviet Union continued to maintain in the postwar era. In fact, she did not maintain as large an army as she might have.

Although Russia did not match America's record for demobilization, she reduced her armies from eleven and a half million men at the end of the War to less than three million eighteen months later. She may have needed an army of this size if she were to consolidate her control over Eastern Europe. Certainly none of us accept the fiction that the people of Rumania, Hungary, Bulgaria, and Poland welcomed Soviet hegemony. Without a large occupying army, Russia would have lost the most precious of the rewards of victory over Germany, control of Eastern Europe, the goal that Russia's rulers had sought for two centuries as essential to her national interest (Morgenthau, 1951).

The conquest of Western Europe would not have served Russia's national interest. Stalin seems to have recognized that maintaining his hold over Eastern Europe would tax Soviet resources to the utmost. Note his willingness to allow Tito to break with Moscow in 1948 despite the fact that he did not need to worry much about Western intervention. He was prescient. As early as 1956, the Hungarian Revolution and rioting in East Germany and Poland challenged Russia's authority. An attempt to absorb Western Europe as well would have posed fantastic problems. As Morgenthau said in 1951 (pp. 161–162):

> The nations of Western Europe have a much stronger tradition of individual freedom, national independence, and cultural achievement than those of Eastern Europe, and they can be expected to be very unruly and unreliable members of the Communist family of nations. Furthermore, the Soviet rulers cannot have forgotten the devastating effects that the first acquaintance with Western civilization had upon the morale of the Russian soldier. If the relatively low standard of living in a country such as Rumania shook his faith in the superiority of the 'Fatherland of Socialism' and

his loyalty to the Soviet cause, the attraction of Frankfurt,
Brussels, and Paris is likely to be much more potent.

It was difficult for America to comprehend Stalin's pursuit
of traditional Russian objectives because the US had long
ago secured the objectives essential to her own national
interest. In the nineteenth century, America eliminated Spain
from Florida, France from the Louisiana Territory, Russia
from Alaska, and Canada became for all practical purposes
independent of Britain. Without another major power in the
Americas, the US enjoyed a sphere of influence that
embraced the entire Western Hemisphere. Its size can be
appreciated by noting that Buenos Aires is as far from
Washington as Paris, and Cape Horn almost as far away as
Moscow.

Having enjoyed such a comfortable buffer zone for so
long, America forgot what it was like to be without one and
was not inclined to sympathize with Soviet objectives in
Korea, Iran, or the Straits. John Spanier (1962) was a
representative American historian of the time. He did not
credit Soviet ambitions with merely the whole of Europe. If
Greece had been lost, the USSR by way of the domino theory
would have inherited the Middle East, South Asia, and
Northern Africa. Can all of Africa and Asia have been far
behind? I suspect that if Greece had been lost and
Czechoslovakia saved, he would have hailed the salvation of
Czechoslovakia as all that stood between America and the
disasters named.

Given Russia's fear of the West, plus her ignorance, she
could hardly be expected to put Western rhetoric about
liberation of the satellites into perspective, much less
statements like that of General Twining, the head of the
Strategic Air Command. He complained that if it were not
for the politicians, he would settle the war in one afternoon
by bombing Russia.

Neither Russia nor the US had much empathy with the
other. Each believed its own account of the origins of the
Cold war without qualification.

## Did it make any difference?

What if America and the USSR had been aware of each other's histories and taken them as minimally sincere? What if the two regimes had been more sophisticated about traditional great power rivalries, and less inclined to believe that they were faced with an opponent bent on world domination?

Some things would have been the same, and some things at least ought to have been the same. By ought to have been the same, I mean that given the vileness of Stalin's Russia and North Korea, expansion of their spheres of dominance should have been opposed on principle. But some things might have been different.

I am assuming that America's sophistication would have included an awareness that left-leaning regimes in Latin America were not necessarily "Communist", even if an unhappy history of American intervention had made them anti-American. Today America is being forced to tolerate the kind of Latin American regimes she consistently deposed or helped depose in the past. If she had controlled her hysteria earlier, she might have let nations like Nicaragua and Guatemala have their own histories. We might have been spared Pinochet in Chile, particularly if the Chilean left had been less anti-American and less influenced by Stalinists (Flynn, 2010). I suspect we would have had something like the Cuban invasion anyway, given Cuba's existence within America's core sphere of influence.

We would not have had the horror of the Cuban missile crisis. Blinded by his perspective, Khrushchev did not realize that no American President could tolerate Soviet missiles 90 miles from Florida (why should they not tolerate missiles near their border when they have put missiles near our border). Most of the American military cared nothing about Khrushchev's room for maneuver (he was simply the enemy). Khrushchev had staked his political life on some sort of concession. Fortunately, Kennedy was conscious of this and gave him a public guarantee that the US would not again invade Cuba and a private promise to eliminate US missiles in Turkey. As to the latter, the press was misled. "Leaks" were arranged insinuating that Adlai Stevenson had been cowardly enough to suggest such a promise and that Kennedy had rejected the suggestion as appeasement. Kennedy assigned Arthur Schlesinger to lie to Stevenson and pretend that the press leaks were not deliberate (Munton and Welch, 2007).

I am also assuming that America's enhanced sophistication would have included an awareness that Asian Communism had indigenous roots, and would reflect cultural diversity rather than become Stalinism with a darker complexion. America might not have intervened in the Vietnamese civil war under the assumption of endless dominos falling, or that nothing worse than a Communist regime could befall that nation. She might not have utterly disgraced herself by supporting a mass murderer like Pol Pot in an effort to dislodge the Communist regime in Cambodia.

I hope that she would have defended South Korea, but that might have been the one thing on the plus side of seeing the world through ideological spectacles. That regime is indeed the worse fate a nation could suffer, and the Korea War was worth the cost. But I am not sure how aware people were of its vileness at the time, and a political realist might have avoided interference in China's traditional sphere of influence. On the other hand, when Communist North Korea was routed, we would not have been so foolish as to approach the Chinese border and bring China into the conflict. She might have intervened anyway of course.

We would not have helped Indonesia liquidate her communists. The tense off-shore island crises between America and China of 1954–1955 and 1958 would not have occurred. America would have recognized the Communist Chinese government much sooner. I should add that why I believe many of these counterfactual propositions will be clearer when we discuss China and Cuba in the next chapter.

However, none of this would have altered the scaffolding that supported the Cold War. Russia would still have emerged from World War II with all the dreams of the Czars dancing before her eyes. And as we have said, no Russian regime could have resisted the lure of control of eastern Europe, a permanently divided Germany, domination of the Straits, a sphere of influence in Iran, and so forth. Given what Stalin was like no America of honor could have countenanced his dominance of Europe. The Marshall Plan, the Berlin crisis, the formation of the opposing alliances of NATO and the Warsaw pact, and the West's cooption of West Germany were inevitable.

The atomic bomb would have been dropped and the nuclear arms race would occurred. Given the awful power of the bomb, and two nations with innumerable points of tension, when in human history would this have led to a successful consummation of disarmament negotiations? I hope no one will name the naval treaty of 1922 that limited the size of the navies of Britain, America, Japan, France, and Italy. This simply froze ratios into place that would have been hard for anyone to exceed in the near future, and what was at stake does not compare to nuclear blackmail.

The termination of the nuclear arms race awaited a sea change in the psychology of either America or Russia. The prerequisites were: (1) A dawning awareness that losing that race would not really mean extermination or being reduced to a vassal state; (2) A vision of a new society that overshadowed the unrelenting effort to compete militarily. It awaited a Gorbachev. More on Reagan versus Gorbachev later.

Events in the Middle East have had little to do with the peculiar psychology of the Cold War. Western sponsored coups have been much like Western sponsored coups of the past. Even the Russian adventure in Afghanistan has Czarist precedents aplenty. US interests in the region are compromised by something entirely new: Israel and US support for Israel. The Twin towers or 9/11 occurred because of Middle Eastern dynamics not American versus Russian dynamics. America's reaction has deep roots that go back to the foundation of the Republic.

The inevitability of the Cold War and the arms race from 1945 to 1965 is depressing. On the other hand, the world we face and its dangers would not be much different had America and Russia been less frantic. We are lucky to have got through the Cold War alive and lucky that its legacy has proved ephemeral.

However, has the Cold War left us any wiser? Our two histories tell us that demonization of an opponent extracts a price: policy based on illusion rather than reality. When we look at America's current war on terror and policy toward Israel, are these any closer to reality than the image of a Greek domino knocking over the Middle East, South Asia, and Northern Africa. Or the specter of Russian troops marching on Paris? But first, let us extract maximum benefit from the history of the Cold War by detailed analysis of selected American decisions.

Chapter 3

# The awesome power of the President

This chapter will analyze the following: the decision to drop the Atomic bomb under Truman; the decision to fortify the off shore islands under Eisenhower; and the decision to invade Cuba under Kennedy. It aims at more than an assessment of whether they can be justified. We want to know how they were made and who was influential. Despite the fact that the last was made some 50 years ago, I believe that the insights they offer have stood the test of time. I have studied more recent decisions, but none of them added much to my understanding of how decisions to utilize force are made.

### The decision to drop the Atomic bomb

Most of those in the Truman administration who held "anti-bomb" views did not flatly reject use of the atomic bomb on Japan. They thought that its use was inevitable, unless Japan could be induced to surrender by other means. However, they held that the bomb should not be used in a way that would inflict massive casualties until the Japanese had been given a demonstration of its destructive potential. For example, dropping the bomb on some symbolic target, perhaps an uninhabited island off the coast of Japan.

## The anti-bomb advocates

The common fear of the anti-bomb advocates was that use of the bomb would engender a terrifying nuclear arms race. In September of 1944, James Connant and Vannevar Bush wrote a letter to Secretary of War Henry Stimson in which they predicted the development of missiles with nuclear warheads (Knebel and Baily, 1963). The following month, scientists in the Metallurgical Laboratory at the University of Chicago sent forward a "Prospectus on nucleonics" that foreshadowed the strategies of nuclear deterrence and first-strike (Smith, 1958). They argued that once America used the bomb against a nation that had no bomb, every nation would feel it needed the bomb so that it would not, like Japan, face a rival who could use it against them at will. Finally, the US would reap a harvest of fear and distrust and others would suspect her intentions and proposals.

It was hoped that prior warning and public demonstration of the bomb would make its use against population centers unnecessary. Political advisers within the anti-bomb group pointed out that there was a peace party in Japan searching for an opportunity to surrender. They hoped that the threat of the bomb plus other factors, such as Russian entry into the war, naval blockade, and an assurance that Japan would not be permanently deprived of her sovereignty, would prompt a surrender. But more important, if Japan refused to surrender despite a public demonstration, America could put the question of the bomb's use on the agenda of the fledgling United Nations. This would create a precedent for international control and relieve the US of the onus of being the first nation to use the bomb unilaterally.

Given our analysis of the origins of the Cold War, it is doubtful that anything would have created an alternative to the arms race, that is, the competition to *acquire* nuclear weapons. But the convention that no one should *actually use* nuclear weapons without UN approval would have been priceless. Imagine that the notion that unilateral use of the any nuclear device was shameful had been cemented into the world's psyche: America would not be disgracing itself today by asserting the right to use "tactical" nuclear devices at will.

A minority of the anti-bomb group flatly opposed use of the bomb. They held that if using the bomb against a nation that did not pose a nuclear threat was immoral, it should not be used in any circumstances. Therefore, a demonstration that carried the implicit threat of use was wrong. The demonstration should occur, but accompanied by a statement that it was intended only to emphasize the gravity of the situation and the necessity for international control. No effort should be made to get UN approval for the bomb's use.

Early on Leo Szilard argued that the very existence of the bomb would provoke a nuclear arms race. Therefore, America should tell the world that the Manhattan Project (the organization to create the bomb) had failed despite enormous effort and expense. He was soon convinced that the secret could not be kept. At that point, he and the other absolute opponents of use found it politic to merge with the majority, and urge public demonstration and UN approval before use.

## Enter Henry Stimson

Most of President Truman's political and military advisers never doubted that the bomb should be used as it was: without prior warning or demonstration and to devastate whole cities. However, among the President's advisers, Secretary of War Henry L. Stimson, played an outstanding role. Despite his disagreement with the case against the bomb, he took pains to understand it and draw it to the President's attention (see Box 3).

His own position throughout the debate is the best account of the pro-bomb argument. Stimson hoped to avoid an invasion of the Japanese home islands. It would entail "an Okinawa" (America lost over 7,000 dead taking this small island) from one end of Japan to the other, that is, an appalling total of dead and wounded on both sides. If an invasion was to be avoided, Japan would have to be shocked into surrendering. The navy and air force held that this might be accomplished by a tight naval blockade and an escalation of the terrible firebomb raids that had tortured Tokyo and Yokohama. Stimson doubted the efficacy of this plan.

---

### Box 3: The last gentleman

Henry Stimson was born in 1867, just after the end of the US Civil War. His career was long and distinguished: Secretary of War 1911–1913 under Taft; Governor General of the Philippines 1927-1929 under Coolidge; Secretary of State 1929–1933 under Hoover; and Secretary of War again 1940-1945 under Roosevelt and Truman. He died in 1950, soon after the start of the Cold War. He would not have been comfortable with the brutal diplomacy that evolved over the next 60 years. In 1929, Stimson abolished the Department of State's code-breaking office, the so-called Black Chamber. He said: "Gentlemen do not read each other's mail" (Stimson & Bundy, 1948, p. 188).

---

More to the point, a prolonged series of firebomb raids would kill more Japanese than taking out a few cities with atom bombs. If the threat of the atomic bomb could be used to shock the Japanese into surrender, it would actually save Japanese lives. Thus Stimson dismissed those who opposed use of the bomb on humane grounds. Recall that the anti-bomb camp accepted the premise that the *threat* of the bomb should be used. This real issue was how to dramatize the destructiveness of the bomb. Stimson was skeptical that a public demonstration would be effective. The Japanese had already refused to surrender after firebomb raids more destructive than the bomb (Stimson, 1947).

What was needed was a psychological shock: watching a city disappear because of one bomb. Dropping the second bomb would raise the specter of a hail of bombs. Stimson also saw practical difficulties in the plan to hold a public demonstration. The original test of the bomb in New Mexico had not been made public because of fear of the fiasco of a dud. What if it did not work when dropped from an airplane? Even if it did, America had only two bombs in stock, and wasting the first would postpone the sharp one-two punch Stimson had in mind for months. During this period, the terrible firebomb raids would continue (Stimson, 1947).

There was a backdrop to Stimson's thinking. Until the collapse of Nazi Germany, everyone working on the Manhattan Project assumed that they were scrambling to beat Hitler to the bomb, and that it was merely a question of who would use it first. The possibility that America would use it on a nation that had no bomb project became real only in late 1944, and it was only then that an anti-bomb group emerged.

## What the President heard: April to May 1945

On April 25, soon after Truman had taken office, Stimson briefed the new President. Stimson had received the Connant-Bush proposal for a public demonstration, and proposed a committee to consider the implications of the bomb and nuclear energy in general (Stimson, 1947). The Interim Committee began to meet almost immediately. Stimson was in the Chair but he saw to it that the committee was not stacked. Its members were: James F. Byrnes soon to be Truman's Secretary of State, William Clayton Assistant Secretary of State, George L. Harrison Stimson's assistant, Ralph A. Bard Assistant Secretary of the Navy, and three scientists, Karl T. Compton and both Connant and Bush.

Initially, the membership can be described as five pro-bomb and three anti-bomb. As we shall see, Bard dissented even more strongly than Connant and Bush.

On May 24, 1945, Stimson received a 10-page letter from O. C. Brewster, a scientist not included in the Committee. He argued that any use of the bomb would make Americans "the most hated and feared people on the face of the earth" and that some demagogue would seek to conquer the world with A-bombs for his "own insane satisfaction".

Stimson was so impressed by the logic of this "remarkable document" that he urged it on General Marshall, Army Chief of Staff, and personally delivered it to President Truman. A few days later, Marshall told John J. McCloy (Assistant Secretary of War) that he strongly opposed use of the bomb without prior warning. He suggested that it first be used against a military target such as a naval base far from population centers. If this failed to bring surrender, the US should designate a number of manufacturing centers and warn the people to evacuate. If the Japanese still persisted, one center would be hit shortly after (Knebel and Baily, 1963).

On May 31, 1945, the Interim Committee held its crucial session. Marshall was present, as well as General Groves, the head of the whole Manhattan Project, and its four scientific advisers, Arthur H. Compton, Enrico Fermi, J. Robert Oppenheimer, and E. O. Lawrence. Stimson (1947) says that careful consideration was given to alternatives such as prior warning and public demonstration but that they were discarded as impractical. From the minutes:

> After much discussion concerning various types of targets and the effects to be produced, the Secretary (Stimson) expressed the conclusion on which there was general agreement, that we could not give the Japanese any warning; that we could not concentrate on a civilian area; but that we should make a profound psychological impression on as many of the inhabitants as possible. At the suggestion of Dr. Connant, the Secretary agreed that the

most desirable target would be a vital war plant employing a large number of workers and closely surrounded by workers' houses (Knebel and Baily, 1963).

Arthur Compton (1956) points out that the three-hour meeting included a one-hour informal discussion over lunch that he instigated at Stimson's table, and that it was during this discussion, that a public demonstration was discarded as impractical. It appears that some, probably including Bard and Oppenheimer, may have sat at another table (Smith, 1958).

We will never know who participated in the lunchtime discussion. The Committee's members endorsed its recommendation without dissent, although this may have been only a show of unity. Certainly, Bard was not convinced as his subsequent behavior reveals. Whether Connant and Bush retained doubts is unknown but they do not appear to have tried to carry the argument further. Marshal, although present, was not a member of the Committee and therefore did not have to endorse its recommendation. Did he carry express opposition at any time after his earlier conversation with McCloy? This is tantalizing because he had the opportunity to argue for his views on two crucial occasions to come.

At this point, Truman had: (1) Heard Stimson's briefing favoring use of the bomb, but which acknowledged the reservations of the anti-bomb group and recommended appointment of the Interim Committee as a consequence; (2) Read O. C. Brewster's 10-page letter urging a public demonstration, delivered in person by Stimson. He may have had one or more conversations with General Marshall who, at this time at least, was strongly committed to prior warning and a purely military target.

## What the President heard: June 1945

The Interim Committee's Panel of Scientific Advisers met separately and on June 16, 1945, it endorsed the Committee's decision. Compton was in the chair and says that they were determined to find an alternative to use of the bomb, but were deterred by the practical difficulties of a demonstration and the possibility that it would not make a sufficient impression on "Japan's warlords" (Compton, 1956). E. O. Lawrence was the last to give in.

Oppenheimer drafted the Panel's report. Subsequently, he emphasized the ignorance of the scientists about the military situation, particularly whether an early invasion of Japan was really necessary if there was no surrender (Personnel Security Board, 1954). The Panel's report notes that some scientists strongly advocate a purely technical demonstration and wish to outlaw the use of nuclear weapons (Stimson, 1947). This is because they had read the Frank Report. Frank chaired a committee of scientists at Chicago's Met Lab and his report gave full statement to the anti-bomb case (Franck Report, 1946).

On June 18, 1945, Truman met with the Joint Chiefs of Staff, Secretary of the Navy Forrestal, Stimson, and McCloy. The invasion of Japan's home islands would be launched on November 1st. They contemplated the appalling casualties, and discussed the A-bomb in the context of trying to secure a Japanese surrender before the invasion date. The question of prior warning was raised, but all were aware of the Interim Committee's conclusion that this was not feasible and that it had been endorsed by the Panel of Scientific Advisors.

McCoy (1953) asserts that no one defended prior warning, an important consideration being fear of a dud. The most fruitful anti-bomb proposal, that use of the bomb be referred to the UN, seems to have dropped out of sight, but presumably fear of a dud was even more damning to its chances. Marshall was present and therefore must have acquiesced, and there is no record that he ever tried to re-litigate the decision.

## What the President heard: July 1945

Ralph A. Bard, Undersecretary of the Navy and a member of the Interim Committee, developed second thoughts about its recommendations. He wrote a letter to Stimson in which he said that he believed that the Japanese were looking for an excuse to surrender, and that prior warning would be sufficient. Although he was assured that Truman had read his letter carefully, he was determined to argue his case in person. On July 1, 1945, he met with Truman at the White House and elaborated his scheme: prior warning was to be accompanied by other measures short of invasion, primarily a naval blockade (Smith, 1958).

Given that Truman had always inclined towards Stimson's views, given his perception of consensus among his advisers, the Joint Chiefs, the cabinet, the Interim Committee, and its scientists, given that so many advocates of prior warning had been won over, Bush, Connant, and Marshall, it is doubtful that Bard's last minute appeal could have shaken him. To fortify him, the very next day, Stimson (1947) sent Truman a final memo summarizing his own plan for achieving a Japanese surrender by dramatizing the destruction that continued resistance would bring. Although the bomb is not mentioned, it was understood that its use would be the dramatic event that would be effective (Morton, 1957).

## What the President decided

At Potsdam, Truman received news of the successful ground explosion of the bomb. On July 17, the President, Stimson, Byrnes, and the Joint Chiefs reaffirmed its use (Truman, 1955). No one raised the question of prior warning (Morton, 1957). On July 24, Truman ordered that General Spatz be ready to drop the bomb as soon after August 3rd as weather would permit. When Japan rejected the Potsdam declaration, he gave his final authorization. Stimson's strategy was successful albeit with some help from the Russians: Hiroshima was bombed on August 6; the USSR declared war on Japan on August 8; Nagasaki was bombed on August 9; Japan offered to surrender on August 10.

As a postscript, the anti-bomb scientists had made one last effort. A bundle of documents reached General Groves (head of the Manhattan Project) on July 25, the day after Truman had cabled his final decision to drop the bomb. It included: petitions from Chicago's Met Lab urging prior warning with 88 signatures; a poll of 150 scientists from the Met Lab with alternatives worded so ambiguously that it was unclear whether a majority favored prior warning or not (Compton wrote a covering letter drawing the latter interpretation); a petition urging prior warning from 68 scientists at Oak Ridge, Tennessee. Truman saw them only after he left Potsdam (Compton, 1956; Kneeble and Bailey, 1963).

## Assessing the decision

I will assess the decision-making process, the merits of the decision, and the President that made it.

**The process**. Had it been up to General Groves, the head of the Manhattan Project, the anti-bomb scientists working under him would have found it hard to inform Truman of their views. Szlilard, Walter Bartky of Chicago, and Harold Urey of Columbia approached Byrnes (Truman's adviser) in May, and when Groves heard of this he was disturbed, apparently feeling they should go through him (Smith, 1958). However, thanks to Stimson's fair-mindedness, most of the anti-bomb camp got through to Truman. It is not clear that the anti-bomb scientists were ever a majority and several of their leaders were won over by Stimson's arguments. The substance of their case would have had to convince Truman and O. C. Brewster's 10-page letter put that case fully. Stimson personally delivered it to Truman as something he must read and consider.

Note how few of Truman's political advisers ever took an anti-bomb position. On the top level, there was only Marshall. He discussed prior warning with Stimson on several occasions culminating in their prolonged discussion on May 29. If he did not argue his case before Truman, it was his own fault. On the second level, Undersecretary of the Navy Bard had a prolonged interview with Truman.

The criteria for a good process I will use are these: the President's advisers formulated all of the alternatives that would occur to a mature moral agent; these alternatives were thoroughly debated; the President was exposed to a reasonable sample of that debate. This decision's process gets a very high mark.

**The merits**. I believe an ideal decision would have been: (1) On August 1, 1945, go to the UN to let them decide whether the bomb was to be used, particularly against a nation that did not have it; (2) The US to cease all hostilities against Japan for a month except those necessary to impose a naval blockade; (3) Be frank about the possibility of a dud and propose that a trial on a purely symbolic target settle this question on September 1; (4) Work hard to produce a third bomb in the unlikely event that the debate, a Russian declaration of war (they would continue to fight against the Japanese armies in China), the public trial (if it worked), and bombing one city (if permitted) did not bring a Japanese surrender.

My ideal decision would not have prevented the spread of nuclear weapons. No one trusted the UN to safeguard its security. Therefore, the USSR needed the bomb so that she would not be at the mercy of the US; China needed it so she would not be at the mercy of the USSR; India needed it after she was humiliated in her border war with China; Pakistan needed it because India had it; Israel needed it because she foresaw the day when she would not have conventional military superiority against the Arab world; North Korea needed it if only because the US seemed inclined to invade wicked nations for their own good and named her as a candidate; France thought she needed it to deter Russia in case the US was unwilling to use the bomb against a Soviet invasion. Only Britain is a clear example of getting the bomb with no rational case. I discount the pathetic case that it helped her get America's ear and substitute her wisdom for new world brashness and naivety.

Nonetheless, the ideal decision would have conferred one great boon: the precedent that the actual use, as distinct from the acquisition, of nuclear weapons must be subject to UN approval.

More important is whether the use of the bomb stains American history with a clearly wicked decision. It does not. Prudent men in that situation might well have decided as they did. When you are in the middle of a war, it takes saintliness to jeopardize an option that may end it, and indeed save enemy lives as well as those of your own troops. Stimson was no saint but he had a strong and coherent case. It is a credit to the decision-makers that there were as many anti-bomb advocates as there were, and that they got the hearing that they did.

**The President**. I credited Stimson for the extent to which Truman heard views contrary to his own but that is only half the story. No President will hear contentious debate unless he is known to tolerate it without reprisal. Members of later administrations used to recount with envy how Truman and Dean Acheson could argue, lose their tempers, pound the desk, and yet remain good friends. Harry Truman was a patriot in the uncomplicated way that an American could be prior to Vietnam. He was not a brilliant man, but he was intelligent, tolerant of dissent, and thoroughly decent (see Box 4).

---

**Box 4: The American patriot with a heart**

After General MacArthur had been dismissed for trying to provoke an all-out war with China, he met President Truman in Washington. He left the meeting stunned. "That little bastard thinks he is the greatest American patriot alive", he said in disbelief, having always assumed that history reserved that role for himself. That Truman was clear thinking and tough enough to dismiss MacArthur, and never wavered in serving his conception of America's interests in the light of a perception of larger consequences, goes half-way to defining the man.

Another incident reveals his humanity. Herbert Hoover was the Republican President in office when the Great Depression struck. He was falsely vilified by Democrats as deaf to the suffering that ensued. In 1945, Truman, a Democratic President, called him to the White House to discuss aid to postwar Europe (later Truman partially restored his reputation by appointing him to head a commission). Hoover left the meeting in tears (Sowell, 2009, p. 133).

---

### Decision to fortify the off shore islands

After Chiang Kai-shek was driven off the mainland of China, he occupied Formosa, now called Taiwan. He also left a scatter of troops on two small islands over a hundred miles distant from Taiwan but adjacent to the Chinese mainland. Quemoy lies outside the harbor of Amoy; and Matsu (or Matsu Tao) and its adjacent smaller islands block the harbor of Foochow (see map).

China bombarded the islands from shore batteries in both 1954-55 and 1958 and occasioned the two "off shore island crises" which alarmed much of the world. However, these crises were alarming only because the islands were fortified in 1953, soon after President Eisenhower took office, and imbued with symbolic significance by that act. As we shall see, the fortification of the islands was an extraordinary event, an occurrence caused by rhetoric that even the rhetorician did not anticipate. The rhetoric was that of Eisenhower's secretary of State, John Foster Dulles.

Eisenhower had no political experience when he took office in early 1953. He relied on two men. Senator Taft would try to get his domestic program through Congress, and Dulles would chart the course of US foreign policy (Goold-Adams, 1962). Dulles never forgot that his power was dependent on the confidence of the President and was careful to clear every major decision with Eisenhower. However, until his death in 1959, he initiated US foreign policy, formulated it, and acted as its public spokesman and chief negotiator (Graebner, 1961).

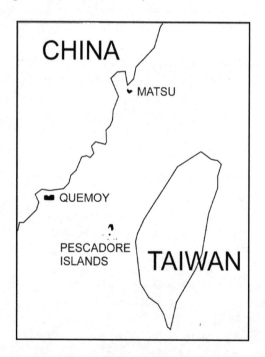

**Map 1. The off shore islands**

## The two promises

Dulles began to work for Eisenhower early in 1952, eight months before the November election. He was preparing the way for a campaign that made two promises: Eisenhower, unlike the Democrats, would end the Korean War; and Eisenhower, unlike the Democrats, would not be soft on Communism. He would cease using the US Seventh Fleet (which patrolled the sea between Taiwan and the mainland) to "shield" Communist China from Chiang's army on Taiwan. The shorthand phrase for this new policy was "unleashing Chiang-Kai-shek".

Dulles served in the Truman administration as a consultant to Dean Acheson the Secretary of State. In March 1952, he created a pretext for his resignation to become Republican Party foreign policy spokesperson in the forth-coming campaign, and signaled the line he would pursue.

At an informal meeting with members of Acheson's Policy Planning Staff, Dulles proposed that if Chiang would reinforce the off shore islands, he should be given a guarantee of US support. He protested against the fact that the US Seventh Fleet was being used to shield Communist China. Stewart Alsop, the distinguished journalist, reported the meeting, but the source was clearly Charles Burton Marshall, a member of the Policy Planning Staff. He was a man much given to talk. Entirely unbidden, he once informed the author about the influence of Kennedy's mistresses on his ambassadorial appointments. He assumes a heroic role in the discussion as reported.

C. B. Marshall objected that Dulles's proposal was in conflict with the whole drift of the administration's policy (Alsop, 1958). This was so. Following Chiang's collapse in 1949, Acheson argued that conflicts of national interest would alienate China from the USSR unless the US drove China into Russia's arms. Fortifying Quemoy and Matsu did nothing to help defend Taiwan from a Chinese attack, and could only be seen as a step toward helping Chiang attack the mainland. This would make China regard the US and not Russia as her main enemy (Acheson, 1949).

Worse, if China decided to invade the islands, they could not be defended without the intervention of the US Seventh Fleet and US troops. America would become involved in a major war over a few worthless islands. Chiang would have every reason to provoke a Chinese invasion in that all out war between the US and China was his only hope of returning to the mainland. As Marshall put it, the US would have committed the classic error of giving a minor ally the power to manipulate US policy for its interests irrespective of American interests. We are told that Dulles greeted Marshall's objections with an icy silence (Alsop, 1955).

What did Dulles have to gain from initiating this conversation? Certainly he knew that he would not convince Truman to fortify the islands. Perhaps he was just trying out his campaign rhetoric to see if it would differentiate the Republicans from the Democrats. He may have been fishing to see if they had any response to his words other than outright rejection.

## Psychological warfare

Dulles did not believe his campaign rhetoric. He did not believe that all one needed to do was unleash Chiang and then enjoy his re-conquest of the mainland. Chiang himself did not believe that. Dulles's real strategy was to inspire in the minds of the Chinese Communist leadership a doubt: that the US just might be prepared to offer massive support to a Chiang invasion if they were intransigent about ending the Korean War. The promise to end the Korean War had to be redeemed because Eisenhower had made it on his advice. In talks with the President-elect in December of 1952, on the cruiser *Helena*, Dulles and Eisenhower agreed that China could be made to see reason only by the threat that America would take the war beyond Korea to China (Spanier, 1962).

On its face the strategy seems absurd. If Americans were weary of the Korean War, how would they react to the prospect of an endless war on the Chinese mainland? And while Dulles liked to talk of "massive retaliation" (using atom bombs on China), this would not actually install Chiang in power but simply make him the most hated man in Chinese history. However terrible the damage to China, it would be nothing compared to the horror of even America's closest allies. Presumably, Dulles was counting on the fact that the Chinese leadership might believe that no rational considerations limited what America might do.

## Did Dulles speed the Korean armistice?

To be fair, once in office, psychological warfare of dubious sanity was fudged with concrete threats somewhat more probable. On February 2, 1953, Eisenhower's State of the Union message did say that the US Seventh Fleet would no longer be employed to "shield" Communist China from Chiang. But less shielding did not necessarily mean anything as extravagant as an invasion. The Seventh Fleet had allowed Chiang to make small coastal raids ever since China had entered the Korean War. In addition, there had been persistent reports, never denied, that the US Navy had helped Chiang maintain contacts with guerillas on the mainland (Donovan, 1956). Therefore, Eisenhower's words committed the US to no more than increased harassment of China's coast by hit and run raids.

As a sign of its resolve to bar a Chinese victory in Korea, in February and March 1953, the new administration authorized increases in the number of US divisions fighting there. On May 22, 1953, the real threat was made. Dulles told Prime Minister Nehru of India that if there was no armistice, the US would bomb Chinese bases in Manchuria, blockade the Chinese coast, and possibly resort to the use of tactical nuclear weapons. The latter threat was made more real by the fact that the US was continuing to equip its air force with Sabre Jets and had moved atomic missiles to Okinawa (Donovan, 1956). Dulles assumed that Nehru would pass his words on to the Chinese Communists. Only two months later, on July 27,1953, the Korean armistice was signed.

Dulles was convinced his threats had worked. There is no consensus on this point (Spanier, 1962, p. 105). China had got out of the Korean War all it could hope to get. They had used it as a convenient excuse to liquidate non-Communist elements in China, and consolidate their prestige by successfully waging war against the greatest of the Western powers. They had replaced Russian influence in North Korea with a Chinese protectorate. Continued pursuit of the war could only divert resources needed for internal development.

## The price of reckless rhetoric

America and the West Pacific nations signed the SEATO Pact in September 1954, an alliance directed against China. China began shelling Quemoy: so much for the theory that Dulles had intimidated her from any confrontation with the US. The world discovered that the off shore islands were now heavily fortified and invested with Chiang's best troops. US officers in uniform were stationed there, and two were killed in the first days of the bombardment. Nothing made sense of this. The threat that the US might fight along side Chiang in some serious invasion of the mainland had never been made, not even through Nehru. Since the only point of fortifying the off shore islands was to add credibility to that threat, it was irrelevant.

This lends support to Alsop's claim that neither Dulles nor Eisenhower directed that the island be fortified. Dulles was aware that during 1953, the CIA had used the islands to help Chiang harass the mainland, small-scale stuff like reconnaissance, guerilla operations, a few air raids. He turned defense of the islands over to the Pentagon. It is doubtful he had anything very ambitious in mind. It is not even clear that the Pentagon's heads, the Chiefs of Staff, wanted anything ambitious. They sent out a Military

Advisory Group (MAG) with the ambiguous orders that they were to help Chiang build up his defenses.

The officers on the spot took these orders literally. Alsop quotes one MAG officer as protesting: "What the hell! We were sent out here to help the Chinese Nationalists build up their defenses, so that is what we did." The Nationalist officers were surprised. They knew the islands were indefensible and privately complained about the intensity of MAG's pressure for a military build-up (Alsop, 1955). However, the fact that the cream of the Nationalist army was moved to the islands shows that one man had kept his eye on the ball: Chiang-Kai-shek. He alone could have welcomed the crises that ensued.

## An American dilemma

The moment the bombardment began, Congress and America's allies demanded to know whether or not the US intended to defend the islands. Dulles's rhetoric had created a dilemma. If Chiang were to evacuate his troops, it would be a public admission that the mainland was gone forever. If his troops faced a Chinese invasion unaided, they would be destroyed. They could not even be supplied in the face of a determined bombardment. Therefore, America had no choice but to say that it would defend them. But to do so would forfeit international confidence in America's whole China policy.

There was a distinction between defending Taiwan itself and defending the off shore islands. Taiwan lay 100 miles off the China coast and was easily defensible. Equally important, America had captured Taiwan and the Pescadores (a near-by island chain) from Japan during World War II. Under the Japanese Peace Treaty, she had the right to occupy them pending their ultimate disposition (Donovan, 1956). Both Truman and Eisenhower had committed the US to their defense.

The off shore islands on the other hand had always been a part of China and were simply a remnant of China still held by the Nationalists. To fight to hold them would be to intervene in the Chinese civil war on the Nationalist side. America's allies fell into two camps: those who agreed with Acheson that America should let Russia assume the role of China's main enemy; those who favored a more aggressive stance but thought the islands indefensible. But both thought that the US irresponsible in letting Chiang fortify them. No one favored a US declaration that it would wage war for them (Goold-Adams, 1962).

## The 1954–1955 crisis

Therefore, when China began to bombard the islands in early September 1954, America could not afford to declare to Congress and the world that she would defend them; and she could not refrain from making such a declaration. The latter would be equivalent to inviting China to invade the islands.

Dulles did a brilliant job of guiding US policy through the horns of this dilemma. He said that while the US had no commitment to defend the islands, it would protect them if an attack on them seemed a prelude to an attack on Taiwan itself. It would of course be entirely up to America to diagnose the intent behind any military action, so Dulles had managed to warn China that any invasion attempt would be repulsed without actually saying so. On December 12, 1954, Eisenhower met with the National Security Council and rejected the views of those who urged a public (explicit) commitment to defense of the islands (Ridgeway and Martin, 1956).

On January 18, 1955, China moved into the Tachen islands and seized Yikiang. These islands are also off the China coast, but they are 200 miles North of Taiwan and had never been fortified. This convinced Eisenhower and Dulles that they must reiterate their non-declaration to defend the off shore islands. Eisenhower sent Congress a special message asking for what came to be known as the "Formosa Resolution". It authorized him to take what steps he deemed necessary to defend Taiwan and the Pescadores. The President emphasized that his authority covered any "localities" against actions that were "preliminaries to" an attack on Taiwan. Dulles drove the message home in a broadcast on February 16, 1955.

In March, China began to slacken her bombardment and at the Afro-Asian Conference at Bandung, Chou En-lai declared that China would not go to war to liberate Formosa, at least not for the time being. The first crisis was over but the absurdity that had created it was still in place and it retained its potential for mischief. The islands were still fortified; Chiang could not evacuate them; and he had secured a mutual defense treaty with the US. It mentioned defense only of Taiwan and the Pescadores, but Eisenhower supplemented it with a personal note to Chiang using the Dulles formula: that if defense of Taiwan required it, the US would help defend Quemoy and Matsu (Goold-Adams, 1962).

## The 1958 crisis

Chiang moved one-third of his army to the off shore islands. Some saw this as an attempt to ignite a full-scale war between the US and China, but he may have been trying only to ensure that the US would not renege on its commitment (Childs, 1959).

China resumed bombardment on August 22, 1958 and on August 28, called on the Nationalist Commander to surrender the islands warning that invasion was imminent. On September 5, Dulles used his earlier language. But to make sure he was understood, two days later the Seventh Fleet, with orders to retaliate if fired upon, began to escort Nationalist supply ships to within three miles of the islands. This was necessary because Chiang's attempt to supply the islands was on the verge of disaster. Chinese guns were decimating his ships. China now backed off fearing to risk a hit on a US naval vessel. More ominous, US marines moved howitzers capable of firing nuclear shells from Okinawa to

Quemoy (Spanier, 1962). The world wondered if a major war was imminent.

China needed a face-saving expedient and on October 21, 1958, Dulles responded by publicly "re-leashing" Chiang-Kai-shek. He and Chiang released a communiqué which again stated that defense of Quemoy and Matsu was part of defense of Taiwan, but also stated that Chiang would liberate the mainland by giving effect to the principles of Sun Yat-sen rather than by force. Actually, Chiang had been restrained as far back as December of 1953 when he promised the US he would not attack the mainland without US permission. But America had never publicly admitted that re-conquest of the mainland was a fantasy. China began to slacken her bombardment and the crisis was over.

What had China gained? From the first crisis, she gained freedom from military harassment of her coast. From the second crisis, a de facto recognition of her existence that paved the way for normalization of relations between America and China a decade later under Nixon. Both of these developments were in the long-term interests of the United States, and marked the fruition of Acheson's China policy. They were almost derailed in favor of what would have been the most counterproductive war in US history, casting even Vietnam and later interventions into the Middle East in the shade. That peril was entirely a product of the mindless fortification of the off shore islands. Without that, even Dulles's heavy-handed policies would have been a bearable interlude.

## Assessing the decision

The decision to fortify the off shore islands was absurd if done deliberately and careless if done inadvertently, in the sense that Dulles took his eye off what was happening as orders went down the chain of command.

**The process.** I will assume the inadvertent scenario, which is far more likely. If the fortification of the islands had been accomplished and publicized in March or April of 1953, it would have played a role in Dulles's strategy to threaten China with enlargement of hostilities should she resist a truce in the Korean War. On the contrary, the project did not get underway until after the June thaw in the truce talks at Panmunjom. And it was done quietly and haphazardly with no public fanfare upon its completion.

It may seem implausible that Dulles allowed Taiwan to drift beyond the horizon of his attention as soon as the Korean War ended; and that officers in the field had a free hand to deal with the fortification of the islands as a purely military exercise. In fact, Dulles's mode of operation makes this hypothesis highly probable.

Dulles carried personal diplomacy to unprecedented lengths, as attested by his 560,000 miles of travel. Emmet John Hughes, Eisenhower's speech-writer and special consultant, says that the American ambassador to West Germany relied on the airmail edition of the New York times for any insight into US policy toward Germany (Hughes, 1958, p. 157). Dulles did not discuss policy with his staff at the State Department and was intolerant of debate or opposition. He wrote all important policy briefs himself, and while he circulated the drafts, rarely allowed a change that did more than polish the prose (Goold-Adams, 1962).

His top assistants were used merely as fact finders. Christian Herter, his Undersecretary of State and successor, lamented:

> It is hard to know what use I am around here, you know. I have been given no authority, and no area of work that is specifically my task. Everyone finds it difficult to know what Foster is either doing or thinking. So . . . I just keep trotting around after events, trying to piece together the true shape of them, so that I can at least be conversant with affairs when Foster is away from Washington (Hughes, 1958, p. 254).

Dulles demanded automatic support. Ambassadorships went to those most ready to toe the line (Gould-Adams, 1962). Hughes (1958, p. 119–120) claims that Paul Nitze's failure to evidence enthusiasm for Dulles's China policy led to his dismissal from his post as chief of the State Department's Policy Planning Staff. Influential under Truman, it became a cipher under Dulles.

Dulles had immense energy, he was efficient, thorough, painstaking, and worked long hours. He had unusual distractions. In 1961, Senator Joseph McCarthy was demoralizing the State Department by purging it of "treason". The Secretary of the Treasury was obsessed with cost saving, and harassed Dulles terribly by trying to cut the State Department's budget. Nonetheless, he simply tried to do too much. George Kennan (1958, p. 40) makes a general accusation of policy drift: that Dulles was bored with Latin America; and allowed the Russian blockade of Berlin to reach crisis point before giving it his attention.

**The President.** Just as Truman was responsible for some of Stimson's virtues, we must ask how much Eisenhower had to do with Dulles's weaknesses. Should anyone aspire to the Presidency who has no coherent view of American foreign policy and no intention of developing expertise? Lacking confidence in his ability to assess, Eisenhower did not want to chair a vigorous debate. He wanted someone to predigest debate and give him a lead.

Eisenhower abdicated the role of authoritative arbiter to a trusted adviser. This created a new decision-making environment, and one with a weakness that renders the adviser likely to perform the role of arbiter worse than a President. The President is secure in his authority, while the adviser's power is derivative. Contrary views that reach the President carry the risk of weakening his faith in your judgment. The peril of debate moves down one level to your advisers. If they are allowed to have independent opinions, and you reject them, what is to keep them from trying to go over your head?

Therefore, you surround yourself with compliant and like-minded men. If you are landed with a subordinate close to the President, someone like Undersecretary Humphries, he is particularly dangerous and must be removed as far as possible from policy discussions. Given the nature of Dulles's role, it was rational to become a one-person decision-making machine. This is not to discount Dulles's character. If someone like Stimson were cast in such a role, he might behave differently. We will never know, of course, but it is indicative that Stimson never tried to become Truman's sole confidant.

### The Cuban invasion decision

Senator Fulbright argued the case against US support for an anti-Castro invasion of Cuba. The US hoped to avoid being held responsible by using Cuban exiles, rather than its own troops, as combat personnel. However, Fulbright knew that this stratagem had begun to fail. There were already newspaper stories that described the exile forces as trained and equipped by the US. On 30 March 1961, he handed President Kennedy a memo (Fulbright, 1963).

Fulbright argued as follows. If the invasion were successful, American imperialism "would be denounced from the Rio Grande to Patagonia". The US might have to intervene to restore public order in Cuba. (What Fulbright seems to have feared was a long-term struggle with pro-Castro guerillas.) She would be blamed for all the defects of post-Castro Cuba. If the invasion faltered, the US might be tempted to commit her own armed forces. As for how to deal with Castro, America should counteract the appeal of his economic reforms through the Alliance for Progress thereby improving the lot of the rest of Latin America.

### *Eisenhower and Cuba*

The only way to explain the appeal of the Cuban invasion decision is to detail its history. By March 1960, Eisenhower believed that Castro was moving toward the Communist bloc. The CIA reported construction projects in Cuba that looked as if they might be designed for eventual use as missile-launching sites. Eisenhower gave the CIA permission to organize exiles from Castro's regime into a force trained in guerilla tactics (Cook, 1961). At this point, there had been no decision to actually use the Cuban exiles (Szulc and Meyer, 1962). However, once the US began to train them, the problem arose as to how they could be disbanded without great embarrassment.

In April 1960, the CIA persuaded President Ydigoras of Guatemala to let them use his nation's territory as a training base. The plan was to train twelve small teams that would infiltrate each province of Cuba, and eventually challenge the Castro regime. Almost immediately, the CIA began to have second thoughts. Castro was building up the strength of his armed forces and they were being supplemented by a large, well-trained civilian militia (Wise and Ross, 1964). They began to plan something more ambitious. By late July, workers were building an airstrip near Retalhulen, Guatemala for an emerging rebel air force. Cuban pilots were recruited and supplied with Second World War B-26 bombers and C-46 transports. Six other camps were opened in Guatemala and some smaller centers in Florida and Louisiana

In October, officials from the State Department, Pentagon, CIA, and White House staff approved a radically new plan. An assault force would invade Cuba, secure a beach-head, and enlarge as it attracted recruits from the surrounding area. On November 4, the CIA ordered that the exile force, now 400 to 500 men, be trained as a conventional army complete with artillery, tanks, and planes (Johnson, 1964). Eisenhower was not informed of the decision, presumably because he was due to retire in a few months and the new President would review all plans.

---

**Box 5: What Kennedy knew**

Ted Sorensen denied that Kennedy was aware of the invasion project. He offers no explanation of how Kennedy's staff managed to remain ignorant of what was widespread gossip among the members of the press corps.

## Kennedy and Cuba

Kennedy had heard that some sort of Cuban exile operation was underway and feared that if the Eisenhower Administration overthrew Castro during the last days of the campaign, Nixon would be swept into office. He phoned a photographer from *Life Magazine* who was shooting pictures of Cuban exiles in training, and was told that there was little chance of an immediate invasion (Wise and Ross, 1964). Kennedy took advantage of the fact that preparations had to be kept secret. On 20 October, he issued a press release stating that the US must strengthen anti-Castro forces, both in exile and in Cuba, and duplicitously accused the Administration of inaction (Freedom of Communication, 1960). See Box 5.

On November 29, 1960, Allan Dulles (brother of John Foster Dulles) gave President-elect Kennedy a briefing about the preparations and Kennedy said they should go ahead. He made it clear that he wanted the option of an exile invasion, but was not ready to decide about its viability. During 1960, Kennedy's attitude towards Castro had changed from sympathy into hostility (Schlessinger, 1965). But he was disturbed how world public opinion would react to US support of an anti-Castro invasion. Incredible as it seems, the Guatemalan airstrips were in full sight of travelers on the Pan American highway (Cook, 1961). In Miami, a reporter was offered the telephone number of the major CIA operative in a public bar (Szulc and Meyer, 1962). By January 1961, both *Time* and the *New York Times* had carried stories replete with detail about US aid. On 28 January, the new President ruled against any overt US participation in the invasion effort (Schlesinger, 1965).

This had military implications. The rebel air force could have only Second World War B-26 bombers. These could be purchased on the world market and Castro had B-26s, so some rebel planes could be presented as defectors. All flights were to take place from Nicaragua rather than US territory. The fuel B-26s consumed on a round-trip from Nicaragua to

Cuba limited them to one hour over the island. In order to give them a full hour, tail guns and gunners had to be eliminated to make room for extra fuel. This made them defenseless against attacks from the rear (Sorensen, 1965). Prop-driven fighters lacked the range for the round-trip, so the B-26s would have no fighter planes for protection. Jets would have signaled US support (Szulc ands Meyer, 1962).

All of this signaled a flight from reality on Kennedy's part. He seems to have actually believed that if the US pretended it was not financing and equipping an invasion force, everyone else would agree to pretend. After the invasion, the world's press identified the pre-invasion stories about the training camps and referred to them with glee. In addition, the CIA was embarrassed by a blunder. It turned out that Castro's B-26s had Plexiglas noses, while the rebel planes did not. The so-called defectors were publicly unmasked.

## The CIA scenario

On March 15, 1961, the CIA chose the Bay of Pigs as a landing site. It had a good airstrip and natural defense provided by surrounding swamps. Air superiority is vital in modern war, particularly when 1,500 men face 200,000. Despite its limitations, the CIA thought the rebel air force might prevail. Two pre-invasion air strikes were to destroy Castro's planes on the ground. This strategy was based on intelligence reports that Castro lacked experienced pilots, most of his planes were obsolete, and those that were operational were not combat-ready. In fact, Castro's pilots performed well. Further, four unarmed T-33 training jets, which intelligence had discounted, had been fitted out with 50-calibre machine guns and converted into serviceable jet fighters (Johnson, 1964; Schlesinger, 1965).

After going ashore, the rebels would seize the nearby airstrip. Henceforth their planes would operate from there and close all highways to the area by incessant bombing and strafing. Within three days, local defectors would have swollen the brigade from 1,500 to 6,500 men. Castro might bring his troops to bear, but riddled by devastating air attacks, they would suffer a sharp initial defeat. Thanks to the "Cuban tradition" of siding with a winner, defections and chaos would break out in his rear. By the end of one week, the rebels would control a large area, and a provisional government would be flown in and recognized as the de facto government of Cuba. It would request whatever US aid it needed (Johnson, 1964).

For the President's benefit, there was a contingency plan. If the invasion foundered, the rebels would "melt away" into the mountains and a publicized defeat avoided. The CIA said nothing about this to the rebels for fear it would lower morale (Schlesinger, 1965). How the Sherman tanks were to melt away into the mountains was unexplained. Castro captured both tanks and men and exhibited them on TV. Since he suffered no sharp defeat, we do not know whether his supporters would have defected. In view of the ferocity with which even the militia fought, it seems unlikely. Among the first killed were three women and two little girls who rushed to the beach to repel the invaders (Johnson, 1964; Wise and Ross, 1964).

## The Joint Chiefs of Staff

What about the military judgment of the Joint Chiefs of Staff? The plan looked better on paper than it worked in practice. The first air strike did leave Castro with only six planes (including two jets). The second strike was called off, thanks to over-optimistic reports of the damage done by the first and Adlai Stevenson's utter humiliation at the UN. He actually believed that the rebel planes were deserters and was undone by the Plexiglas nose blunder. Contrary to expectations, Cuban militia were in the area and contacted Castro who brought troops and planes to bear within hours. It was Castro who had the advantage of air superiority. His jets sank or drove off all four of the rebel freighters, which meant the loss of most of their ammunition, food, and medicine (Johnson, 1964).

With better luck, the rebels might have held a beach-head for a week. It is doubtful they could have much enlarged it, and the scenario of large scale defections to their ranks looks fanciful. Here the Joint Chiefs made no independent prediction. They said that success was contingent on defections, and deferred to the CIA as the experts on its likelihood. Both Schlesinger (1965) and Sorensen (1965) speculate that despite Kennedy's statements to the contrary, the Joint Chiefs thought that he would be pressured into committing troops if events brought him face-to-face with failure. They were mistaken. On April 12, Kennedy told the press "that there will not be, under any conditions, an intervention in Cuba by the United States armed forces". That afternoon the President told a meeting that the US would not recognize a rebel government unless it was firmly established.

## Kennedy and his advisers

The politically sophisticated decision-makers, the President and his advisers, should have appreciated Fulbright's point: that even if the invasion was a success, it would gravely damage America's political image and burden her with micro-managing post-Castro Cuba. During March and early April, they held seven or eight meetings and listened to the CIA spin its fantasies.

Some were more realistic than Kennedy about who would be held responsible for a venture so obviously sponsored, financed, and equipped by the US. Schlesinger opposed the plan in a private conversation with Kennedy and submitted three memos. Chester Bowles sent Secretary of State Dean Rusk a memo and asked to see the President. Rusk filed the memo away and gave Bowles the impression that the invasion might be no more than a guerilla infiltration (Schlesinger, 1965).

The pivotal April 4 meeting included Dulles and Bissell from the CIA; Rusk and Thomas Mann from the State Department; McNamara and Paul Nitze from the Department of Defense; General Lemnitzer of the Joint Chiefs; Schlesinger, Adolph Berle, and McGeorge Bundy; and meeting with the group for the first time, Senator J. William Fulbright (Szulc and Meyer, 1962). Dulles outlined the CIA's final plan. Kennedy pointed his finger around the table for comment. Neither Schlesinger nor Rusk spoke up. Others supported the plan with minor qualifications.

The only man who tried to argue down the CIA in open debate was Fulbright. He rehearsed his arguments at length; until then, only the President had heard him. He was incredulous at the apparent unanimity. He emphasized that the risks were wildly out of proportion to the threat Castro posed for the United States (Schlesinger, 1965).

Kennedy retired to make his decision. Pundits were measuring him against the legend of Franklin Delano Roosevelt, and his domestic reforms would not be nearly as spectacular as Roosevelt's. A foreign policy coup might capture the public's imagination. As one member of the Administration put it to the author: "We felt we had done some fancy dribbling, but that we needed some baskets."

Kennedy believed that the press would accept America's pretence of non-support. If the rebels collapsed, it would be just another Latin American coup that had flopped and the story dropped in a few days (Sidey, 1964). Dulles kept saying that the exiles could filter away into the mountains and escape capture and publicity. He also stressed the "disposal problem". What was to be done with the Cuban exile force if it was not used? Were they to go back to Miami and tell newsmen that the Administration had prevented them from attacking Castro? As Louis J. Halle (1961) pointed out, Kennedy would be more vulnerable to domestic criticism for actually stopping an anti-Castro movement than simply omitting to launch one.

Fulbright's admonitions had to contend with the fact that everyone else endorsed the CIA's plan. The unanimous consensus of men with whom the President had met for a month opposed the objections of someone he had first seen a few days before. On April 7, 1961, Kennedy decided in favor of the invasion (Schlesinger, 1965; Sorensen, 1965).

## *Fiasco and aftermath*

The invasion was launched on Monday April 17. Castro's trainer jets made short work of the exile B-26s. By the end of Tuesday, only four were operational and the rebels were on the verge of defeat. Around 2 a.m. on Wednesday morning, the President ordered the only exception to his veto on the use of US forces. The aircraft carrier Essex could furnish air cover for one hour at dawn while supply ships tried to unload, and the remaining exile B-26s made another attack. This turned into a fiasco. The B-26s arrived an hour early and without cover from US fighters, two of the three planes that reached the invasion area were shot down (Johnson, 1964; Schlesinger, 1965).

On Wednesday, Kennedy vetoed sending in the Marines and blockading Cuba (Sidey, 1964). He ordered American destroyers, with cover from US jets, to evacuate what was left of the brigade. He was too late. With the rescue fleet an hour or two away, Castro captured the remnants of the exile force (Johnson, 1964).

## *Assessing the decision*

To paraphrase Cyrus Sulzberger, the Cuban invasion decision made Americans look like fools to their friends, rascals to their enemies, and incompetents to the rest (Spanier, 1962). The great disposal problem was no problem at all. You call off the invasion and give the rebels the option of being dropped as guerillas or trained as infiltrators. If they go back to Miami, they are men who shirked a chance to liberate their country. If the press whines about the invasion being called off, you ask who it was that blew cover and made anything more ambitious impossible.

**The process.** Arthur Schlesinger had no doubt about who was to blame. As Secretary of State, Rusk should have articulated Fulbright's arguments. He says that Kennedy put a high value on receiving a variety of advice, and was disappointed that Rusk was so reticent. This leaves the behavior of at least one person, Arthur Schlesinger, unexplained. Why then, rather than sitting in silence, did he not make his President happy by speaking up and refuting the CIA point by point?

Schlesinger's comments on Rusk are remarkable for the use of saccharine to coat poisonous pills of invective. He has exceptional intelligence—and an irrevocably conventional mind. He is vigilant—but insulated from the real world by a screen of clichés. His speeches have quiet authority—although the world dissolves into a montage of platitudes. He suffers, "no doubt", from fears of his own inadequacy. Sadly he is incapable of offering an opinion on any important issue. Others have defended Rusk as an active adviser and efficient executor of the administration's policies (Opotowsky, 1961).

Schlesinger's praise of Kennedy is embarrassing. At times, it seems tongue-in-cheek, for example, his eulogy of the President's speech defining US policy towards Castro in

---

### Box 6: Schlesinger and the junior officers

Schlesinger's book, *A Thousand Days*, is remarkable for the amount of space devoted to the war records of various officials. They are "the junior officers of the Second World War come to responsibility", a description that may not endear them to those who served in the ranks during that conflict. More than once, their combat experience is cited as the source of their virtues. For a particularly hair-raising example, see page 260.

the wake of the invasion failure. The speech's chief merit, it seems, is that Schlesinger could not understand just what Kennedy was getting at. Concerning the President's advisers (all but Rusk), he borders on satire when extolling their flexibility and courage (Schlesinger, 1965). See Box 6.

**The President.** If Kennedy failed to get advice, he may have had only himself to blame. *US News and World Report* (1963) quotes the usual Washington insider: "It is a waste of time to try to find the top advisers to the President on policy matters. They simply do not exist. The President himself and his brother Robert run the show, along with a battalion of yes men."

Kennedy sent Rusk plenty of signals as to the kind of Secretary of State he wanted. Before he offered Rusk his job, the President appointed an Under Secretary of State, an Assistant Secretary of State, the US Ambassador to the United Nations, and other lesser officials. Rusk knew that strong Secretaries of State had demanded the right to suggest their own men leaving the President with essentially a veto power. He could be excused if he felt that his position was an anomalous one. Sorensen (1965) says that Kennedy liked Rusk for being low-key, and could not have got along with a strong-minded Secretary of State like Acheson.

Hugh Sidey (1964) matches Schlesinger in his adulation of Kennedy. Yet he detects extraordinary sensitivity to criticism. Kennedy read the papers and tested every word and every phrase for friendliness, dissected them with scientific precision to determine the degree of approval or disapproval. A reporter, whose paper had said that the White House staff was badly organized, got a phone call from the President himself: I hear you bastards have done it to me again, followed by a stream of vituperation. When Kennedy got angry at the *New York Herald-Tribune* for its coverage of his dispute with US Steel, he cancelled the White House's 22 subscriptions.

Sorensen (1965) believes that when presented with the CIA's invasion plan, the President's advisers feared they would be labeled as cowards if they opposed the military. When Sorensen first heard of the meetings, Kennedy told him, with an earthy expression, that too many of his advisers seemed frightened by the prospect of a fight (he said that they had no balls). If that attitude communicated itself to the President's advisers, there is no mystery why they kept silent. There is no mystery why the only man who dared speak up was a Senator, someone who did not depend on the President's tolerance for his position.

The Cuban invasion decision was taken less than three months after the Kennedy Administration took office. In the first three months, no cabinet officer or adviser knows what his President thinks of him well enough to feel secure. The Cuban invasion decision was the first hurdle they had to clear in the race to see who would gain the President's confidence and become one of his confidants. My own view is that Kennedy was a little too much of a king, Rusk a little too much of a courtier, and the Administration a little too new. Together, these factors added up to something nearer court politics than Presidential decision-making.

I must add that that Kennedy learned from the Cuban invasion failure. Sidey (1964) reports that he was so concerned over how the decision-making process had worked that he directed his brother to look for defects. At the first National Security Council meeting after the invasion failure, Robert Kennedy observed that fear of the President inhibited honest comment, and noted the need for better communication. Over the next year things much improved. Witness Kennedy's mature handling of the Cuban missile crisis in 1962.

## The decisions collectively

None of these decision were vicious. History has yet to see the nation that makes no mistakes. Even the worst decision, the Cuban invasion decision, was largely a symptom of the Cold War psychology in its heyday.

During the first 20 years of the Cold War, America tended to think of all nations that were not Communist, except the most stridently neutralist, as part of the West. Between 1945 and 1965, no Communist nation had abandoned Communism and four nations, China, Czechoslovakia, North Vietnam, and Cuba, had turned Communist. America tended toward hysteria. The balance sheet showed nothing except losses, and every nation that went Communist was counted as an irreparable loss. This hysteria extended to Castro's Cuba, and any regime in Latin America that was left-leaning was diagnosed as suffering from an illness that might prove fatal. Fulbright could not understand why Castro loomed so large as to blind the Kennedy administration to the risks of the Cuban invasion. It was like asking the Spanish inquisition why it was so hysterical over one heretic. Heresy may spread and every heretic that dies a heretic is a soul lost forever.

### The awesome power of the President

The most important thing that emerges from these decisions is that the President really is respected as the Commander-in-chief of the Armed forces, as the person mandated by God (or at least the Constitution) to decide when the United States should use force outside its borders.

His power is limited in the sense that he cannot do something that totally outrages the intellectual elite that thinks about foreign policy and can articulate its opinions. If he decided to invade Canada, questions would be asked about his sanity. His negative power, his power to veto a foreign adventure, is far closer to absolute than his positive power. Even here there are limits: Roosevelt could not have vetoed declaring war on Japan after Pearl Harbor; Kennedy had to get Russian missiles out of Cuba; and Bush probably had to try to extract Osama bin Laden from Afghanistan after the 9/11 attack on the World Trade Center.

However, these cases all involve either an attack on the United States or an initiative by an enemy state that gave her a dramatically increased capacity to launch such an attack (Russian missiles in Cuba). If Truman had held strong views about setting a precedent for UN approval of the use of nuclear weapons, he could have taken that path and vetoed use of the bomb in the meantime. If Eisenhower had been committed to the China policy of the Truman administration, the notion of fortifying the off shore islands would have been under a permanent veto. If Kennedy endorsed a Latin American policy that allowed that continent to settle its own affairs, so long as this presented no military threat to the United States, he could have vetoed the Cuban invasion.

As for subsequent decisions, the President certainly had the power to veto sending US troops to Vietnam, the invasion of Iraq, and the attempt to nation build in Afghanistan after the collapse of the Taliban regime. He has more room for maneuver than many think over America's relationship to Israel. This is grounds for cautious optimism: better presidents promise better policies, particularly if the world-view of America's foreign-policy thinking elite alters.

# PART II

## The Transition

Chapter 4

# Vietnam and Pol Pot

The first great trauma that converted many Americans into post-national people was the American intervention that prolonged the Vietnamese civil war. I will discuss why it was easy for America to get involved in Vietnam, why it was almost impossible to get out, and how national honor became a razor's edge that bitterly divided opinion. This last was a gradual development. As every other rationale for the war slipped away, national honor expanded to fill the vacuum. For those whose commitment was unshakable, their patriotic zeal was fanned by outrage at the vacillation of their fellow citizens. For those who came to see national honor as a vehicle to justify mass slaughter, it suddenly imploded. It became a false God that had to give way to a higher morality.

### The way in

French Indochina consisted of Vietnam, Laos, and Cambodia. The Japanese conquered the area during World War II but in 1946, France resumed control. The Viet Minh demanded independence and initially fought a guerilla war in rural districts. In 1949, the Chinese Communist regime began to aid the Viet Minh. After the Korean War reached stalemate in 1951, and was terminated by the armistice in 1953, Chinese aid escalated. America supplied military aid to France and eventually was paying 75 percent of her costs. By 1953, the war had become a conventional war between two armies equipped with artillery and modern weapons. The

French position deteriorated steadily culminating in the siege of their stronghold at Dienbienphu in March 1954. By early April, the French were desperate and asked for an air strike by US planes from aircraft carriers.

## Dulles and Vietnam

Secretary of State John Foster Dulles searched for someway to retrieve the situation. He was implacably opposed to the expansion of Chinese influence in Southeast Asia (Adams, 1962). Admiral Radford, chairman of the Joint Chiefs of Staff, argued that an air strike would be sufficient to relieve the French. The rest of the Joint Chiefs demurred and said that troops would have to be committed as well. Dulles privately thought that they were correct and planned a strategy: get permission for an air strike alone; after it fails argue that America's prestige is at stake and that therefore, troops must be committed to turn a public failure into success.

Dulles went to Congress hoping for a joint resolution authorizing an air strike, a resolution that would commit the Democrats as well as the Republicans to the ground war that would ensue. The Democrats realized what was up and asked what America's allies thought. Britain strongly opposed what they saw as another Korean War to save the French (this is perhaps the one benign influence that Britain has ever exercised on US policy). At this point, Eisenhower vetoed the air strike. This was crucial because his prestige was such that had he made a public plea for intervention, Congress would have granted his request (Roberts, 1954).

Dienbienphu fell and French resistance ended. On July 21, 1954, the Geneva Conference divided the country into North Vietnam under the Viet Minh and South Vietnam under an emperor, who was soon displaced by his Prime Minister Ngo Diem. Dulles found what solace he could in salvaging South Vietnam from Communist control, and in the formation of the SEATO alliance as an instrument of defense against further expansion of Chinese influence. (Adams, 1962). The Geneva Conference also stipulated that nationwide elections be held in 1956 to unify the nation. However, Diem refused to enter into negotiations with North Vietnam about the administration of these elections. By 1959, insurgents allied to the North (called the Vietcong) began to fight for his overthrow.

## Vietnam and China

Why was a Communist Vietnam so much to be feared? As early as 1948, it was clear that one Communist nation could cherish its independence from another. In that year, Tito defied the USSR and declared Yugoslavia a nonaligned nation. When Kennedy took office in early 1961, the bitter division between Communist China and the USSR had become public: the Chinese were referring to the Soviet leaders as "The Revisionist Traitor Group". Vietnamese history is a veritable record of fierce commitment to independence from China. Between 1255 and 1285, she repelled invasions by the Chinese as well as three invasions by the Mongols.

The absurdity of the cold war psychology was demonstrated from the day the Vietnamese Communists attained victory in 1975. Immediate tensions with China culminated on November 3, 1978, when the USSR and Vietnam signed a twenty-five year mutual defense treaty directed against China. In 1979, Vietnam and China fought a bloody border war with heavy casualties on both sides. This is not hindsight. As early as 1954, those familiar with Vietnamese history spoke of a Communist Vietnam as a Yugoslavia in gestation.

## Kennedy and China

Despite all of this, it never occurred to Kennedy that the best bulwark he could have against Chinese influence in Southeast Asia would be a united and strong Communist Vietnam. Whatever his differences with Dulles, the Cold War psychology with its Communist versus non-Communist balance sheet was Kennedy's psychology. He was equally committed to the equation that to contain China in Southeast Asia was equivalent to containing Communism.

The first evidence of Kennedy's thinking on China consists of speeches delivered in 1949 when he was a 32-year-old Congressman, then in his second term in the House of Representatives. These speeches were most unfortunate. They questioned the loyalty of those responsible for the loss of China in a way that was to become only too common. Kennedy is said to have regretted his comments a few years later, and to have lamented that he ever made them (Schlesinger, 1965).

Ted Sorensen, who was the President's most trusted adviser, is perhaps the best source of Kennedy's views on China during his Presidential years. Sorensen (1965, p. 665) quotes an off-the-record remark Kennedy made in 1962: "These Chinese are tough. It isn't just what they say about us but what they say about the Russians. They are in the Stalinist phase, believe in class war and the use of force, and seem prepared to sacrifice 300 million people if necessary to dominate Asia."

Sorensen goes on to say that the President saw no way of persuading the Chinese to abandon their aggressive designs short of a patient, persistent American presence in Asia. It would be a mistake to attempt to conciliate China. Any American initiative towards negotiation or diplomatic recognition would merely convince the Chinese that aggression paid.

Kennedy did hope for improved relations in the long run. Once China saw that aggression did not pay, new leaders and internal problems would persuade her to accept peaceful coexistence. At that time, normalization between China and the West would become possible (Sorensen, 1965).

## *Kennedy and Laos*

Kennedy's first military intervention in Southeast Asia was in Laos. The Eisenhower administration had spent some $300 million there, most of it in support of General Phoumi who was rightwing and pro-Western. The Communist Pathet Lao controlled the northern part of the country and aided by a Soviet airlift, they routed Phoumi's forces. Early in March 1961, Kennedy faced the prospect of Communist domination of the whole country and warned Russia and China that the US was prepared to intervene.

In a strategy meeting on March 9, Kennedy tentatively agreed to a 17-step plan of increasing military intervention, moving from military advisers up to an all-out commitment of US troops if necessary. One unit, including guerilla experts and helicopters, was sent to neighboring Thailand. On April 20, American military advisers in Laos were ordered to wear their US uniforms as evidence of America's determination to commit its own troops. In May, the combatants agreed to a cease-fire and there followed a yearlong series of negotiations at Geneva. By the next spring, fighting had broken out again and in May 1962, the Communists advanced almost to the Thai border. Kennedy sent navy units and two air squadrons to the area, and 5,000 US troops were landed near the Thai border. Australia, New Zealand, and Britain also sent units (Sorensen, 1965).

In June, the parties at Geneva managed to agree on a coalition government headed by a neutralist. Although the crisis passed and US troops were withdrawn, the coalition government proved unworkable. The Communists were afraid to come to the capital, which was patrolled by General Phoumi's troops. The settlement really amounted to a de facto partition of the country with the Communists still in control of their bailiwick in northern Laos.

## *Kennedy and Vietnam*

During his first days in office, Kennedy also faced a deteriorating situation in South Vietnam where the Viet

Cong guerillas were gaining in strength against the pro-Western Diem government. The President set up a special task force with representatives from his White House staff, State Department, Defense Department, and CIA. It called for an immediate commitment of US troops, but Kennedy was cautious by temperament. He merely tripled the US military advisers in Vietnam, which until then had numbered only about six hundred, and gave them permission to accompany government forces in combat.

In September 1961, the Viet Cong seized a provincial capital. Now all of the President's major advisers agreed that the US should commit troops. They argued that even a small force would boost the morale of Ngo Dinh Diem's army and discourage the Viet Cong. Kennedy was ambivalent. He feared that American troops might become bogged down in Vietnam as the French had, and that European troops would alienate the people. On the other hand, he feared to be thought unwilling to stand firm against Communist expansion. Sorensen (1965, p. 654–655) is worth quoting:

> Formally, Kennedy never made a final negative decision on troops. In typical Kennedy fashion, he made it difficult for any of the pro-intervention advocates to charge him privately with weakness. He ordered the departments to be prepared for the introduction of combat troops, should they prove to be necessary. He steadily expanded the size of the military assistance mission (2,000 at the end of 1961, 15,500 at the end of 1963) by sending in combat support units, air combat and helicopter teams, still more military advisers and instructors and 600 of the green hatted Special Forces.

Kennedy was assassinated on November 22, 1963 and Lyndon Johnson became President. Despite apologists who are "certain" that Kennedy would have allowed a Communist victory in South Vietnam rather than commit more and more troops, we will never know the truth. As the situation deteriorated, he would have come under strong political pressure to intervene. Many were poised to echo the young Kennedy, and castigate those who lacked "the resolve" to save South Vietnam from Communism.

Shortly before his death, Kennedy did issue an order to cut the number of US troops by 1,000, an order that was immediately rescinded by Johnson. Nevertheless the troops he committed during his final year were numerous enough, and visible enough, so that an America withdrawal, followed by a Viet Cong victory, would make it harder for a Democratic President to be re-elected.

Kennedy was responsible for initiating the use of chemicals in South Vietnam. They were used for a full decade, between 1961 and 1971, to destroy rice crops and defoliate large areas the countryside. About 12 million gallons of Agent Orange were sprayed over forests and the Mekong Delta. The current Vietnamese government estimates there are over 4,000,000 victims of dioxin poisoning in Vietnam. The US denies any conclusive link between Agent Orange and the Vietnamese victims (Failoa, 2006).

However, the Veterans Administration lists prostate cancer, respiratory cancers, multiple myeloma, type II diabetes, B-cell lymphomas, soft tissue sarcoma, chloracne, porphyria cutanea tarda, peripheral neuropathy, and spina bifida as conditions found in the children of American soldiers exposed to Agent Orange. Even today, these chemicals affect the Vietnamese landscape, cause disease and birth defects, and poison the food chain. In some areas, dioxin levels remain at over 100 times the accepted international standard (Agent Orange, 2008).

### No way out

If Kennedy's China policy was one of containment rigidified by ideology and tempered by caution, Johnson's was one of containment influenced by indecision. However, Johnson's indecisiveness was not that of a Hamlet, but that of a master politician. Unfortunately, he faced a problem no politician could solve.

## Who was Lyndon Johnson?

Johnson was the archetype of the politician described in Plato's *Republic*. He was someone for whom politics, and the popularity a political career engendered, was the source of self-esteem. He was also the most astute of a kind of politician peculiar to America, one whose career was based on negotiating compromise after compromise. He was particularly noted for his successful "courtship" of powerful figures that could advance his career (see Box 7).

---

### Box 7: Lyndon Johnson and Sam Rayburn

In 1952, when I was 18, I served Sam Rayburn as a valet. He was a heavy drinker and in the evening, he often presided over a court attended by Texas Congressmen. Rayburn at that time was the very powerful Speaker of the House of Representatives and Johnson a freshman Senator, although newly appointed majority whip. His posture towards Rayburn was reverential: "Boy, fill Mr. Speaker's glass."

---

Between 1936 and 1964, a conservative coalition of Republicans and Southern Democrats controlled Congress and refused to pass the welfare legislation desired by the President who was usually a liberal. The President in turn vetoed the conservative legislation that got through Congress. American political scientists call it the era of stalemate. If government was to function at all, the leadership in Congress had to negotiate compromises that were minimally acceptable both to the conservatives in Congress and the liberal in the White House. Therefore, Congress bred a group of politicians with a genius for negotiating Southern conservative–Northern liberal compromises. Often these men came from states on the border between North and South, hence the name, border-state politician.

Johnson's years in Congress were from 1937 to 1961, an almost perfect match for the era of stalemate. His awareness of the nature of his role is reflected in his reply when, while serving as Majority Leader of the Senate, he was asked to define his political philosophy: "I am a free man, an American, a United States Senator, and a Democrat, in that order. I am also a liberal, a conservative, a Texan, a taxpayer, a rancher, a businessman, a consumer, a parent, a voter, and not as young as I used to be nor as old as I expect to be – and I am all these things in no fixed order" (Johnson, 1958). You can hardly beat that for bridging the dichotomies in the body politic unless someone, a hermaphrodite perhaps, could add that he was both a man and a woman.

## Johnson and his advisers

The most striking characteristic of Johnson's policy was that he refused to commit himself to any of the three schools of thought that prevailed among his advisers. Whenever possible, he took steps on which most of his them could agree. Therefore, we must describe the views of the military, the State Department, and Congress.

First, there were military men like Admiral Radford whose aims were victory, the elimination of the Viet Cong, and permanent US military bases. They held that a showdown with China was inevitable. Therefore, the sooner it came the better. At present, the US had an immense advantage in striking power, while eventually China would become a full-fledged nuclear power. This then was the time to consolidate American influence in Southeast Asia, and South Vietnam must be made into a bastion of American military strength (Baldwin, 1965).

The second school of thought dominated the State Department. Their aim was a South Vietnam most of which was controlled by the present government and home to US military bases. They agreed that containment of China required a military balance of power in Southeast Asia. Since the Chinese military presence to the north was so overwhelming, America had to maintain a military presence in countries that were pro-Western enclaves. Where the government was able to maintain its own authority, as in Thailand, the US military presence could remain off shore on the decks of the Seventh Fleet. But if the government were in danger of falling, as in South Vietnam, the US must set up bases on the mainland itself.

Therefore, the US must send enough troops to accomplish three objectives: US bases must be rendered secure; the major cities, the Mekong delta, and the central highlands must be pacified, so that the South Vietnamese government could become self-sufficient in policing these areas; and vital avenues of communication must be kept open so that the cities would not be starved into submission. While the Viet Cong need not be eliminated, they must be reduced to a manageable rural insurgency (Rusk, 1966).

The third school was just a collection of individuals with some area of agreement, journalists like Walter Lippmann or Senators like Fulbright. Their aim was a neutralized South Vietnam, with no military bases, and a new government with which the Viet Cong would be willing to co-exist. They believed that the present South Vietnamese government would never be able to dominate most of its territory. They saw only two possibilities: either a permanent US military presence, which would be engaged in never ending large-scale combat; or negotiations with the Viet Cong toward a political solution. The only rationale for sending US troops was to convince the Viet Cong they could not win an outright victory. They would then accept what would be in effect a Laotian solution. They would retire to their rural strongholds, have de facto control there, and console themselves with the fact that they had eliminated all foreign military presence from Vietnamese territory.

Right from the start, Johnson tried to avoid a definite choice between these three policies. All schools agreed that the number of US troops should be increased and during

1964, he allowed the minimum expansion that would satisfy them, that is, 15,500 troops became 25,000.

In March of 1965, America began bombing North Vietnam in a campaign that eventually deluged the North with a million tons of missiles, rockets and bombs. The American Commander, General William Westmoreland, described the situation as critical. He was convinced a massive investment of American troops could win the war within two years. Johnson accepted Westmoreland's assessment of the military situation, and increased US troops from 25,000 to over 200,000 troops by the end of 1965. But he left it unclear as to whether this was a step toward victory, or pacification of the areas nominally controlled by the Saigon government, or a prelude to negotiations. (U.S. Department of Defense, 1969; Karnow, 1983; McNamara et al., 2000).

Westmoreland could not deliver. Even though his requests for more and more troops were met, the number eventually increased to over 550,000, progress was not evident and US casualties were high. American soldiers were being killed at the rate of over 1,000 a month throughout both 1967 and 1968. Johnson continued to play his advisers off against one another. American troops were to sweep the countryside, a concession to those who contemplated victory. But when sweeping the countryside, they usually aimed at keeping the Viet Cong off balance rather than at occupying their territory, a concession to those who want U.S. troops to play a limited role. And all the while, he paid verbal homage to those who wanted a negotiated settlement, statements that he would accept any government in South Vietnam that the people choose, presumably a government elected after a negotiated armistice.

When he had to make decisions, Johnson always tried to find the middle ground. For example, he refused to perpetuate a pause in the bombing of North Vietnam as Fulbright urged; but he also refused to escalate by bombing Hanoi and Haiphong as the military advocated. Rather, he resumed bombing but continued the practice of avoiding population centers.

## Reality polarizes America

Johnson's instinctive strategy of reconciling his advisers was leading him to disaster. Broker politics works if you can reconcile every party that has the power to veto the compromise solution. When Johnson reconciled his advisers, one party, with an effective veto, was not at the table. All three groups assumed that the Communists could be ignored or at least coerced into a compromise they hated.

They all believed that America could win a test of wills with an enemy that was fighting for the unity of its nation, just as Lincoln had fought to preserve the union during the US Civil War. America was fighting in another country 9,000 miles away to preserve a bundle of illusions. It was fighting to contain Communism when it was really trying to contain Nationalism (which is not to deny that the nationalist crusade was being led by Communists). It was fighting to serve national interests that did not exist. It was fighting for a national honor that was becoming more and more compromised in the eyes of many of its people with each passing day. It was fighting so it would not have to admit to a mistake that had killed thousands of US troops. This was an unequal contest and it was predictable whose resolve would give way first.

As the conflict persisted, Johnson's advisers began to enter the real world, but in doing so, they drifted so far apart that they became irreconcilable. After America had invested its army and prestige in Vietnam, there were only two realistic policies: use overwhelming military force to win an outright victory; or concede defeat disguised as much as possible by face-saving expedients.

The stark reality of this choice was what made the way out of Vietnam so difficult. What was at stake was the myth of American invincibility. The Korean War had shocked Americans. They thought of their country as one that had never lost a war, one that had beaten the forces of Japan and Nazi Germany combined (Americans have never tended to dwell much on the roles played by their allies). It seemed inexplicable that a mere decade later America could not easily defeat the armies of China, or even North Korea. That the Truman administration pursued a "no win" policy, held back from using nuclear weapons for "political" reasons, was infuriating particularly as casualty lists grew (Tang Tsou, 1963). However, at least the Korean War was a stalemate and South Korea had been preserved for the West. Vietnam aroused even more powerful emotions. Non-victory was bad enough but surrender and the acknowledgement of defeat was unthinkable. It was an affront to very core of national honor.

The catalyst was the Tet offensive of January 1968 in which the Viet Cong and North Vietnamese Army occupied most South Vietnamese cities. It was a military failure but a propaganda success. It did not provoke a general rebellion by South Vietnamese civilians, and their troops were dislodged within a month with heavy losses. From this point on, North Vietnamese regulars became the majority of the Communist forces fighting in the South. Significantly, the morale of the army of the Saigon government, never high, suffered. Desertion rates rose from 10.5 per thousand before the Tet offensive to 16.5 per thousand by mid-year (Arnold, 1990; Duiker, 1981).

The scale and audacity of the effort dismayed the American public. Only two months previously, General Westmoreland, still the commander in the field, had said he was "absolutely certain" that the Communists were unable to mount a major offensive (Weiss and Dougan, 1983). US soldiers continued to die at a rate of more than one thousand per month throughout the remainder of 1968.

### Victory versus surrender

Those who still sought victory included General Westmoreland, now Army Chief of Staff, General Earl

Wheeler, Chairman of the Joint Chiefs of Staff, and Clark Clifford, soon to be Secretary of Defense, although Clifford defected shortly after taking office. Just before he relinquished command, Westmoreland said that an additional 10,500 troops were desperately needed.

Wheeler encouraged Westmoreland to ask for whatever troops he needed, and told Johnson that 207,000 more were a military necessity. The Joint Chiefs were concerned that US troop strength had fallen throughout the world and wanted another 200,000 troops stationed in the US as a strategic reserve. National mobilization would be necessary to achieve these numbers, that is, 1,200,000 marine and army reservists would have to be called to active duty (Dougan and Fulghum, 1985; Karnow, 1991; Tucker, 1999; Zhai, 2000).

Those who were gradually reconciling themselves to surrender were more numerous and even the mainstream press began to move in that direction. On February 27, 1968, the influential Walter Cronkite closed a broadcast called *Report from Vietnam* with an editorial comment:

> To say that we are mired in stalemate seems the only realistic, yet unsatisfactory, conclusion. On the off chance that military and political analysts are right, in the next few months we must test the enemy's intentions, in case this is indeed his last big gasp before negotiations. But it is increasingly clear to this reporter that the only rational way out then will be to negotiate, not as victors, but as an honorable people who lived up to their pledge to defend democracy, and did the best they could (Cronkite, 1968).

## Johnson decides

On 27 February, Johnson discussed the proposed troop increases with the Secretary of Defense. They would require an extra 200,000 men and an extra expenditure of 25 billion dollars over two years. Johnson did not believe America would accept mobilization of the reserve and this level of spending. Yet to deny the request, would signal to the Communists that America had set limits on its military intervention, and even Westmoreland and Wheeler granted that those limits held no prospect of ending the military stalemate (Johnson, 1971).

The next day Johnson appointed a group to make a complete policy reassessment. Clark Clifford became Secretary of State on March 1 and was appointed to head the group. Clifford had always been a member of the victory faction but now he changed his mind. He wanted the President to limit the US troops in Vietnam to 550,000 men and then gradually force the Saigon government to take over the fighting. He found allies in Paul Nitze (Deputy Secretary of Defense), Paul Warnke (Pentagon International Security Affairs), Phil Goulding (Assistant Secretary of Defense for Public Affairs), George Elsey (Presidential adviser), and Air Force Colonel Robert Pursely (Clifford and Holbrooke, 1991).

He found an even more potent ally in public opinion. After Tet, college students burned draft cards and chanted, "Hey, hey, LBJ, how many kids did you kill today?" The President became virtually a prisoner in the White House, and the Secret Service did not allow him to attend the 1968 Democratic National Convention because of the danger posed by protesters. Senator Eugene McCarthy entered the 1968 election campaign as an anti-war candidate. On March 12, in the New Hampshire primary, McCarthy won 42 per cent of the vote to Johnson's 49 per cent, a humiliation for a sitting President trying to win the endorsement of his own party. On March 16, Senator Robert Kennedy of New York entered the race. On March 31, 1968, the President announced he would not seek or accept the nomination of the Democratic Party for another term (Johnson, 1968).

Thus Lyndon Johnson forfeited everything that had given his life purpose. He died not quite five years later, two days after what would have been the end of his second full term.

Once Johnson realized his political career was over, the broker politician finally chose sides between the three

groups, now utterly passé, who had been his advisers. On
October 31, 1968, he announced that he would order a
complete cessation of air, naval and artillery bombardment
of North Vietnam should the Hanoi Government be willing
to negotiate. He had finally sided with the group that was
prepared to accept a negotiated neutral Vietnam. That he did
so after five years of indecision probably made no difference.
This group had been no more in touch with the realities of
Vietnam than the others that vied for his support.

## Prerequisites for surrender

Even those reconciled to withdrawal and a possible
Communist victory wished to salvage as much of the myth
of US invincibility as they could. They needed three things to
make defeat acceptable: the Saigon government must show
that it was *unworthy of salvation* by clear evidence that it was
unable to guarantee its own survival; the concept of an *exotic
war*, a once in a century piece of bad luck, a strange war that
no nation in the history of the world could have won; and
since it is clearly a mistake to enter a war no one in history
could win, a *scapegoat.*

## Nixon and Vietnam

Johnson provided the scapegoat. Nixon had the advantage
that no one could blame him for taking America into
Vietnam. As to whether the war was actually unwinnable,
we cannot be certain. If Nixon had been willing to reap the
whirlwind by mobilizing the reserves, increasing the US
troop presence to 750,000, destroying much of North
Vietnam by bombing its dikes, maintaining the effort for
another five years, virtually taking over the Saigon
government to run an uncorrupted army, the country might
have been secured for the West. Left to itself the Saigon
government gave what Americans considered ample
evidence that it could never be reformed. All three of the
prerequisites for surrender were in place.

This is not to say that anyone announced that America was prepared to accept surrender. There had to be a face-saving way out. This was Nixon's policy of "Vietnamization" of the war, slowly withdrawing US troops with the Saigon government taking over responsibility for its own defense. But implicit in the strategy was that if the Saigon government failed, that was that. And when the crunch came, America was prepared to write off its 58,000 dead and a decade of struggle; and was prepared to tolerate Communist domination of South Vietnam.

For a time, the military strength of North Vietnam (and the depleted Vietcong) versus the Saigon government with US support was evenly balanced. The pattern was that whoever undertook an ambitious offensive operation suffered.

In February 1971, the Saigon army attacked the route North Vietnam used to send troops and supplies to the South through neighboring Laos (the Ho Chi Minh trail). They retreated in disorder and half of them were captured or killed, partially because of the incompetence of their officers. During 1971, US troops were reduced to 200,000 and began to suffer from morale problems. In a few cases, enlisted men assassinated officers by throwing grenades into their tents (Karnow, 1991; US Army, 2005).

During the 1970s, the North received one billion dollars or more annually in Soviet aid. In March 1972, the North Vietnamese and Vietcong launched their own offensive armed with modern artillery and armor. It was a disaster. They made some gains in the Mekong Delta, but their troops sustained heavy losses and were beaten back thanks to overwhelming US air support. The US also stepped up the bombing of North Vietnam. The fact that US support in the field and air cover were crucial did not bode well for the future

In 1973, Vietnamization of the war became a reality. In January 1973, the Paris Accords were signed and stipulated a ceasefire, elections, and withdrawal of US troops within 60 days (See Box 8). Only the last actually occurred: American ground troops left in March 1973 and bombing missions ceased in August. In June 1973, Congress passed a bill that required Congressional approval of funds for military action in Southeast Asia. Subsequently, US aid to the South fell from 2.5 billion dollars annually to 0.7 billion in fiscal 1975 (Bibby, 1985; Tucker, 2000).

---

### Box 8: Kissinger and Joseph Heller

Henry Kissinger, played a dominant role in US foreign policy from 1969 to 1977, and received a Nobel Peace Prize for his role in negotiating the Paris Accords. Others took a dimmer view of his role during Vietnamization of the war.

In Joseph Heller's novel *Good as Gold*, the Jewish protagonist (Gold) thinks that Kissinger is too wicked to be a Jew. He treasures the occasional photo in which Kissinger is shown eating a ham sandwich. When Kissinger is replaced, Gold phones his (fictitious) successor to gloat. The new Secretary of State makes some pious remark about pretty big shoes to fill. Gold says, come on, he was no Metternich or Castlereagh. The new architect of US foreign policy says, "Who the hell is Metternich, and who the hell is Castlereagh?"

---

In late 1973, the Saigon army launched its last offensive, an attempt to seize Communist bases along the Eastern seaboard and in the Mekong Delta. The North Vietnamese and Vietcong counterattack repulsed them and occupied additional territory hitherto under Saigon control (Bibby, 1985).

*Ford and Vietnam*

On August 9, 1974, when Nixon resigned under threat of impeachment, Gerald Ford became President. He witnessed the North Vietnamese offensive that ended the war. In March 1975, they easily captured a provincial capital in the Central Highlands. Saigon ordered their forces to withdraw, and what began as a reasonably orderly retreat soon degenerated into a panic. City after city fell and the North Vietnamese closed on Saigon. The South Vietnamese 18th Division made a valiant stand just north of Saigon but after a week, they were overwhelmed. By April 27, the North Vietnamese had encircled Saigon and on April 30 1975, their tanks broke through the gates of the Presidential Palace (US Army, 2005)

Major Thomas Bibby of the Marine Corps University Command and Staff College has written the best analysis on why the Saigon army collapsed.

On paper, even at the beginning of 1975, the Communist army was no match for the government army. The latter had 1.1 million men under arms as compared to 160,000 North Vietnamese troops operating in the South. But over 90 percent of the Saigon forces were in non-combat units, while all but 44 percent of the North Vietnamese were in fighting units (supplemented by remnants of the Vietcong). Probably the two sides had the same number of combat troops, about 100,000 each.

But this too gives a false impression. In the Saigon army, many held command because of political connections or military appointments they had purchased. There was money to be made. There were "ghost soldiers": superior officers would pocket the salaries of men who had been killed or had deserted by not taking them off the payroll. There were "roll call soldiers": men would appear only for roll call and give their salary to their superiors in return for being allowed to be absent from duty. This, of course, meant that when units had to go into combat, they were found to be severely under-manned (Bibby, 1985).

Setting aside under-manned units and incompetent commanders, corruption undermined morale. The families of soldiers had too little to eat while their commanders spent time in Saigon enjoying lives of luxury. The draft was utterly corrupt. Deferments were granted arbitrarily, and those unfortunate enough to be conscripted did not have a limited tour of duty. They had to serve until killed or disabled. Those trapped in their units felt they were a minority expected to bear the entire burden of the war. Draft dodging and desertion reached epidemic proportions. Some commanders were simply cowards. General Phu, commander of the Second Army Corps, ordered his troops to defend their region to the death, and then fled (without informing his subordinates) by helicopter to Saigon (Bibby, 1985).

**A question of honor**

Thomas Sowell (2009) believes that the Tet offensive in 1968 offered a forfeited opportunity. Had not opposition to the war weakened America's national resolve, she could have won the war and preserved her national honor. The Tet offensive was indeed a military blunder and badly depleted the ranks of the Vietcong. But let us see what America would have had to be resolved to do.

*The three steps to victory*

First, not only sweep jungle areas but also leave US troops in place to hold them, which would have necessitated raising troop levels to 750,000. Even in 1969 (long after Tet) US troops killed totalled 11,600. If it took another five years to secure these areas, that would have added 58,000 American dead to the 46,000 killed up to that time, for a total of over 100,000. More intensive fighting would have also meant many extra South Vietnamese dead.

Second, since North Vietnam was happy to send in troops to make good the shortfall of the Vietcong, the US would have had to break the resolve of the North by "bombing her back to the Stone Age". Rummel (1997) puts civilian deaths from the bombing that was done at 65,000. Perhaps 200,000 would have done the trick?

Third, the US would have had to do what no President contemplated doing: conquer South Vietnam and depose the Saigon government. The latter simply could not mobilize its citizens into a battle-worthy army. America would have had to administer the draft, appoint the officers, take the roll calls, make sure the troops were properly paid, ensure that no military supplies went astray, and run a court system with jurisdiction over all cases of corruption. Even after her troops left, she would have to run the Government military machine for some years treating South Vietnam as a virtual colony or conquered province.

## In retrospect

And what would have been the point of all of this: national honor. By 1968, national honor was no longer a unifying concept. The war had divided Americans into traditional patriots for whom national honor was still enough, and those for whom it no longer was. Only a fragment of the latter had generalized their opposition into a coherent post-nationalist moral stance. But the seeds were planted. For many Americans, perhaps a million or so, national honor had become a prima facie principle to be overridden by considerations of humanity. For them the day of automatic patriotism was over.

Who today thinks that the present Vietnamese government is a threat to American security? Was there ever sufficient difference between the South and North Vietnamese regimes to justify either the tactics of defoliation or the scale of the killing? My estimate of lives lost in Vietnam is 1.75 million broken down as follows: South Vietnamese army 266,000; Communist forces 1,100,000

(mostly killed by US troops: Sowell, 2009, p. 248); US forces
58,000; other forces 7,000; civilians 316,000 (90,000 by US
military action). As this reveals, American intervention
accounted directly for about 55 percent of the deaths or
almost one million. Was it really wrong in 1968 to decide
against another half million dead?

---

**Box 9: The war after Tet**

**South Vietnamese Army and US Army deaths compared**

|      | S. Vietnamese | United States | US percentage of total killed |
|------|---------------|---------------|-------------------------------|
| 1966 | 12,000        | 6,100         | 34 %                          |
| 1967 | 13,000        | 11,200        | 46 %                          |
| 1968 | 28,000        | 16,600        | 37 %                          |
| 1969 | 22,000        | 11,600        | 35 %                          |
| 1970 | 23,000        | 6,100         | 21 %                          |
| 1971 | 23,000        | 2,400         | 9 %                           |

*Source: Wikipedia (2010)*

---

It might be argued that the war could have been won at
less cost than I have estimated. However, the notion that the
communists were on the verge of defeat in 1968, and that the
Saigon army needed only a bit more help to secure victory, is
false. As Box 9 shows, through all of 1968 and 1969, for a full
two years, the war was still prosecuted vigorously.
American forces still played their usual prominent role,
suffering over a third of the casualties and inflicting most of
the enemy casualties. Shifting the burden to the South
Vietnamese Army did not get underway until 1970. If the
Communists were really fatally wounded by Tet, the war
would have been over by then.

Sowell notes that the end of the war did not stop the
killing. Hanson (2001) says the some 50,000 to 100,000 boat

people died trying to escape. I have seen higher estimates. I never thought the ending the war would end the killing. Rather I thought that settling scores after such a bitter civil war (no matter who won) would mean a bloodbath. However, at least the killing did not stay at 100,000 per year for an additional five or ten years.

### America and Pol Pot

There was also an insurgency in Cambodia. In 1975, Pol Pot and the Khmer Rouge assumed power and began mass murder. Thanks to delusions of grandeur about recreating the ancient Khmer empire, which once ruled over all of Southeast Asia, Pol Pot repeatedly attacked Vietnamese territory. In 1979, the Vietnamese invaded and installed their own regime in Phnom Penh. Pol Pot fled but consolidated his forces near the Cambodian-Thai border.

I was disturbed by the fact that America continued to recognize Pol Pot's regime as the legitimate government of Cambodia, but excused this as a largely symbolic gesture directed against the new Communist Vietnam. After all, only France broke ranks among America's allies. Despite scattered reports, I could not bring myself to believe that America was supporting and maintaining Pol Pot for reasons of real politic.

However, in 1989, Strobe Talbott (1989) published a piece in *Time*, and I had no choice but to believe. *Time* was hardly a left-wing outlet, and I had found Talbott's previous stories reliable. He was later associated with Yale University and served as the Deputy Secretary of State from 1994 to 2001. The next year put the final nail in the coffin of doubt. The *New York Times* published their review of the Peter Jennings special, "From the killing fields" that aired on ABC television on April 16, 1990 (Goodman, 1990). Collectively, Strobe and Jennings made four assertions.

(1) **The two regimes**: Pol Pot unleashed a holocaust of killing. The Vietnamese army that expelled him plundered the almost empty capital of Phnom Penh and carried the

goods on trucks back to Vietnam. However, the regime they established, the PRK or People's Republic of Kampuchea, was surprisingly moderate.

(2) **US policy**: After the USSR and China fell out, the former backed North Vietnam while the latter backed Pol Pot. The US considered the USSR the greater enemy. Therefore, she collaborated with the Chinese in an effort to replace the North Vietnamese sponsored regime in Cambodia with a tri-party alliance inclusive of the Khmer Rouge. Both sources quoted Zbigniew Brzezinski, Carter's National Security Adviser, as saying in 1981: "I encouraged the Chinese to support Pol Pot. Pol Pot was an abomination. We could never support him. But China could." He added that the US "winked semipublicly" as the Chinese funneled arms to the Khmer Rouge, using Thailand as a conduit.

(3) **US assistance**: The US did not leave assisting the Khmer Rouge entirely to its Chinese ally. William E. Colby, the former Director of Central Intelligence, and Congressman Chester G. Atkins, Democrat of Massachusetts, agreed with aid workers on the spot that Prince Norodom Sihanouk, the putative leader of the coalition of anti-Government forces, was in fact a puppet of the Khmer Rouge (Sihanouk said that the Khmer Rouge had reformed and praised their efficiency on the battlefield). Jennings states without qualification that American arms were finding their way to Pol Pot's forces and that the latter were dominant. The CIA estimated that the Khmer Rouge had more guns than the two non-Communist guerrilla groups that the US had been aiding openly.

(4) **US motives:** The accusation is not that the US liked Pol Pot, rather it is that preventing him from butchering his way back to power just did not count for much. Aside from the pursuit of what was seen as America's interests, there is the suspicion that US opposition to Vietnamese influence in Cambodia was a symptom of her humiliation by North Vietnam in the Vietnamese war. Congressman Atkins characterized US policy as "a policy of hatred."

Having established the credibility of these assertions, I will amplify them:

## (1) The two regimes

The French Communists were anti-intellectual and saw uneducated peasants as the true proletariat. They selected Pol Pot for rule partially because he kept flunking his university courses. It was sad that he was not a simple agrarian, but at least his mind was relatively uncorrupted by learning. Pol Pot shared their preference for peasants. In 1975, his first official act was a forced march (with four to five hours warning) of all three million people resident in Phnom Penh to rural areas with no sustenance provided. The elderly or sick that could not walk were shot. From 1975 to 1979, all city dwellers were forced to relocate to rural collective farms and forced labor projects. The goal was to "restart civilization in Year Zero" (Kierman, 2002).

Those now resident in rural areas were classed as either full-rights people or depositees (former city dwellers). The later were marked for death: their rations were reduced to two bowls of rice soup per day. A combination of slave labor, malnutrition, poor medical care, and executions resulted in the deaths of an estimated 1.7 to 2.5 million people, approximately one-fifth of Cambodia's population of 8.0 million. This did not disturb the Khmer Rouge. They announced that only one or two million people were needed to build the new society. As for the other six million: "To keep you is no benefit, to destroy you is no loss." Hundreds of thousands were taken out to dig their own graves. Khmer Rouge soldiers beat them to death with iron bars or hoes or buried them alive. Bullets were not to be wasted (Kierman, 2004). Enough.

In contrast, the PRK regime that the Vietnamese installed in 1979, headed by Heng Samrin, qualified as the best regime possible within the limits imposed by Communist ideology. The Khmer Rouge still controlled much of the countryside and they devastated rural areas under government control, for example, they systematically destroyed all stores of rice. When the PRK came to power, the new government was greeted with famine, and no schools, books, hospitals, police, courts, civil service, mail, telephones, radio, or television (Vickery, 1984).

In the decade after 1979, the new government literally built a society from scratch. Famine was eliminated only after a partially effective campaign against the Khmer Rouge by the Vietnamese army in 1984 to 1985. A new administrative and technological elite was educated. Except for the Chinese, who were considered a reactionary influence, the regime showed respect for Cambodia's ethnic minorities whether Thai, Vietnamese, Cham or Montagnard. Buddhism, carefully controlled, was revived and by 1985, Buddhist festivals began to be celebrated. The overwhelming majority of the people welcomed the new regime, not because they wanted a puppet government, but because they wanted sanity. The government created displays of Khmer Rouge atrocities and used slogans such as "We must prevent the return of the former black darkness" (Slocomb, 2004).

After 1989, spurred by the collapse of Communism in Eastern Europe and by popular demand, Cambodia began to dismantle its Communist regime. The name Cambodia was resurrected, it called itself a neutral and non-aligned state, restrictions on religion were lifted, Chinese New Year celebrated, the economy liberalized, and "only" eight students shot when they rioted against corruption. In 1993 the UN supervised elections that restored Sihanouk as king (Marston, 1997).

Since then the ruling party has been consistently re-elected. It has genuine support but many of its votes are the result of state patronage and government control of the state media. A private opposition press is tolerated and criticizes the government vigorously but it has a limited readership. Economic growth has been healthy and the population has doubled to 14 million. The corpse that Pol Pot left in his wake has been resurrected. This is what America put at risk, preferring the prospect of more "black darkness".

## (2) US policy

America wished to overthrow the PRK because Vietnam was an ally of the USSR, and the less Vietnamese influence in South East Asia, the less Russian influence. What exactly could the USSR hope to gain from the aid she gave to Vietnam? All she got out of aiding Castro's Cuba was a steady drain on her finances, but at least she almost got missiles of strategic significance 90 miles off the coast of Florida. Does anyone believe that the fiercely independent Vietnamese would have tolerated a Russian military presence on their territory, after their enormous sacrifices to get rid of first the French and then the Americans?

Even if Russia had got a base of operations, it would have driven the Chinese crazy, and America would have got an eternally faithful ally, just as she now had a temporary one. The US went into Vietnam worrying about a Communist Vietnam as a vehicle of Chinese influence into South East Asia; now she was concerned about Russian influence. Both fears had in common only that they were absurd. Would Russia have got "good will"? Well so what, but even this was unlikely. The Russian are not good guests. When they went to Egypt to build the Aswan dam, they despised the food, the climate, the laziness of Egyptians, including the pilots and soldiers they ordered about, were angry when denied alcohol, and worst of all, did not tip. The dislike was heartily reciprocated (see Box 10).

The only thing that the US was denying Russia in Vietnam was unpopularity. All that was at stake was the most trivial kind of point scoring. Since the USSR wanted one side to win, America must give the Russians a black eye by helping the other side, even if this meant backing Pol Pot.

---

**Box 10: The Russians and their African colonies**

In 1945, America missed a wonderful opportunity when the USSR demanded the Italian colonies in Africa. If she had handed them over, the Cold War, as far as the developing world was concerned, would have been won before it started. The spectacle of Russians hanging on to power and shooting blacks all over Africa would have made American race relations seem benign.

---

*(3) US assistance*

It is not disputed that America entered in a joint arrangement with China in which the Chinese role was to revive and rearm the Khmer Rouge. After Pol Pot was defeated, and his forces regrouped near the Thai border, the US told Thailand to treat them as needy refugees. They were given "humanitarian" aid (fed, healed, and sheltered), which was very helpful. Thailand did not need much persuading as she was making money from the weapons China sent to the Khmer Rouge. The joint effort was effective. By the mid-1980s, the Khmer Rouge had amassed about 35 to 50 thousand troops and cadres. Pol Pot had announced his retirement, but was in fact nearby and still in charge.

What is controversial is Jennings's claim that American arms were finding their way directly to Pol Pot's forces. Here I rely on a report by the journalist Anthony LoBaido (2010) that originally appeared in *World Net Daily*. This is a conservative publication whose authors include Pat Buchanan, David Limbaugh (brother of Rush Limbaugh), and Bill O'Reilly. The article contains interviews with several military personnel. Tom Berta was with 374th Tactical Airlift Wing. "We ran guns into Cambodia, lots of guns, 50 flights a day in July and August. The CIA exercised what it called the 'Third Option' and sold arms to the Khmer Rouge". Nina Morrison, a former pilot with the CIA front company Air

America, refused to undertake any flights used to arm and supply the Khmer Rouge.

Retired US Special Forces Major Carl Bernard told *World Net* that Special Forces point man U. K. Pappy was the most knowledgeable about US aid. The most damning quotation: "I learned for sure at this time that all supplies sent to the Cambodian forces were to be split between the pro-West forces [of King Sihanouk] and Pol Pot. The State Department didn't want to be unfair, just in case Pol Pot took the country back." His suspicions were aroused by shipments of arms that kept getting "lost". On one occasion, he called the US Embassy and asked a top official whether these arms were going to Pol Pot and just why they had disappeared. The official asked for his name and serial number. Pappy sums up: "I know personally that the US was giving material aid to Pol Pot, right along with the pro-West Cambodians."

It is no surprise that the Khmer Rouge emerged as the best-armed and most effective fighting force. They received $100 million a year from China alone, while the other groups averaged at best $25 million between them. The US was of course well aware of the growing Khmer Rouge dominance.

## (4) US motives

As for the accusation that US officials were sulking over the loss of Vietnam to the Communists, I find imputing motives distasteful. Even when one individual seems largely responsible for a decision, like John Foster Dulles, I prefer to confine myself to describing what I think to have been his strategy to serve US interests as he saw them. It is hard to divine even one's own motives, which is a good reason for extending charity to people you will never meet.

Take Brzezinski whose words seem so lamentable. His career as a whole is not that of a wicked man and it is worth noting that he later opposed the invasion of Iraq. Only individuals have motives. A complex interaction of decision-makers, such as the one that formulated policy towards Pol Pot, does not have a motive; but it does set goals. One oddity. Brzezinski was National Security Adviser under President Jimmy Carter, the self-proclaimed champion of human rights. I have yet to find an adequate analysis of what Carter knew and condoned in regard to Pol Pot.

## A prolonged conversion experience

The fact that US intervention prolonged the war in Vietnam and cost an extra million lives shook many Americans. There had always been some who were immune, those motivated by an internationalist ideology or pacifism or humanity. But after 1970, there was something new: a large number of perfectly ordinary Americans unwilling to follow the flag wherever it was planted.

I was less disturbed by Vietnam than by its aftermath. The war itself did not show that the US decision-making system had produced something beyond the pale of morality. No one anticipated how long the killing would last. At any given moment, the military were convinced that the next escalation would bring victory. Many of those killed were enemy combatants who, from the US point of view, had merely to lay down their arms to survive. Most important, once US casualties had mounted, it was political suicide for Johnson to simply acknowledge that the war was a mistake and withdraw. It took a notoriously anti-Communist president who did not have to own the war to end it.

None of these considerations meant that citizens should not have opposed the war and tried to terminate it. But the Vietnam war could be looked upon as an aberration, rather than an event that necessitated a shift of fundamental loyalty to something beyond my nation state. I was blinded by American exceptionalism: other nations might be responsible for great wickedness but not America.

I tried to find extenuating circumstances for America's actions in Cambodia. Perhaps the policy elite thought that any one of the three factions they were supporting might become dominant and that therefore, there was only a one in three chance of Pol Pot's return. Perhaps there was a contingency plan to overthrow him if he did. Nothing worked. Throughout this period, American officials refused to allow his regime to be described as genocidal. They simply did not want Americans to know the truth. America was playing dice with genocide for a prize no higher than scoring a meaningless point in Cold War competition. This was too much. The fact had to be faced: the US political system could produce great wickedness as a *goal*, as distinct from causing great suffering as an *unforeseen consequence*.

Therefore, on April 26, 1990, two days before my 56th birthday, I became immune to the tug of automatic patriotism. On that day, I did not think through the full consequences or wear the label of "post-national person". These were developments that occupied the next 20 years.

But I did know that national honor had to be abandoned for something else. I began to think about the concept of civic virtue: a willingness to defend your nation because of its quality of life and the fact that its quality of life produces just behavior on the international scene. It is true that an elite may disproportionately influence foreign policy. However, a healthy society does not engender an elite capable of great wickedness. Just as something corrupt produced Stalin and his henchmen, something corrupt, rather less corrupt of course, produced US officials willing to support Pol Pot. In any event, I was no longer naïve. I was psychologically prepared for the inhumanity that was soon to mark US policy in the Middle East.

Chapter 5

# *America, Israel, and the Middle East*

Moral assessment of America's behavior in the Middle East is central to our concerns. But before we can judge, we must understand and that means describing US and Israeli policy in the context of history. Finally, it is not enough to describe and condemn. We must illuminate the causes of US and Israeli behavior, if only to convince their citizens that they can do otherwise.

Therefore, I will discuss five subjects. (1) *Objectives*: Both the US and Israel are attempting to perpetuate Israel's nuclear monopoly in the Middle East, which compromises America's role as enforcer of the Nuclear Non-proliferation Treaty. (2) *The tide of history*: The modernization of the Middle East will make this objective impossible. (3) *Moral questions*: Can the US sanctions against Iraq prior to the Iraq war be defended, and what of the war itself. (4) *The first behavioral hypothesis*: Israel's self-image blinds her to her true interests. (5) *The second behavioral hypothesis*: The affectionate ties between Jewish and non-Jewish Americans, within the US opinion-making elite, have caused America to subordinate her own interests to the perceived interests of Israel.

## Objectives: Nuclear weapons and Israel

The Nuclear Non-Proliferation Treaty became operational in early 1970. It recognizes the existence of five nuclear weapon states: America, Russia, Britain, France, and China. There are four nuclear nations who are not signatories, namely, Israel, India, Pakistan, and North Korea (whose capacity at present is probably limited). Although these four are not liable to the treaty provisions, there is an expectation that they will behave as if they were, for example, that they will give nuclear technology to non-nuclear states only for peaceful purposes (and subject to safeguards such as inspection).

There is also an expectation that the non-signatory nuclear powers will not behave like "rogue states", that is, that they can be trusted not to use nuclear weapons to threaten their neighbors or aggrandize themselves at their neighbor's expense. America has capitalized on that expectation by assuming the role of a sort of world sovereign, one that has the right to determine who can legitimately possess or acquire nuclear weapons. North Korea, Saddam's Iraq, and Iran have been rejected; India, Pakistan, and Israel, have received their licenses. Since Israel refuses to confirm or deny the existence of her nuclear capacity, her license is a tacit one. The rest of the international community is split on Israel's case. In September of 2009, the conference of the International Atomic Energy Agency called on Israel to adhere to the treaty and accept inspection. The resolution passed 49 votes to 45 with 16 abstentions. The Israeli delegate stated that Israel would not co-operate in any way with this resolution (Keating, 2009).

America's stance is simple: that Israel is a non-aggressor state and therefore in effect in compliance with the treaty. The position of Syria, Iraq (under Hussain), and Iran is also simple: that Israel is an aggressor state, witness her continual annexation of territory on the West Bank of the Jordan; that her nuclear monopoly in the Middle East is maintained so that she can expand with impunity; and therefore, that they have the right to break that monopoly, even though they may have to pretend that they are not acquiring weapons thanks to American pressure. In response, America's stance is that the mere fact that these states are anti-Israel renders them rogue states.

## Israel's right to exist

This question of Israel's right to exist is non-resolvable because both sides have an unbeatable moral case. If I were a Jew at the end of World War II, after the Holocaust and betrayed by virtually everyone, I would have wanted my own nation state. Even if I faced the fact that this would mean some displacement of non-Jewish people, I would have said: "Who has ever built a nation without inconveniencing someone; is Israel supposed to be the first nation in history that is different?" And if I were a Palestinian, I would have said: "But we did not do anything; are we alone to suffer for the world's crimes?"

Once you have a legitimate moral case both for and against Israel's right to exist, endless attacks on Israel and endless retaliations are both justified without quibbling as to who may have gone too far. Lack of empathy follows as a matter of course. The Israeli says, "we just want to be left in peace", and the Arab says, "while keeping (and expanding) what you have seized from me."

To put the Arab position into perspective, imagine the unimaginable. The Romani (gypsies) spent the thousand years between 250 B.C. and 750 A.D. in the Punjab on the border between what is today Pakistan and India, arriving in Europe about 1300 A.D. After Nazi attempts to exterminate them during World War II, they return to the Punjab and carve out a state called Romani. We will assume that they arrive in a northern India divided into Islamic states. Their displacement of Muslims and their own religion make them anathema. America gives huge sums to Romani and Romani becomes the predominant military power in the region with formidable nuclear weapons. America denies nuclear weapons to any hostile power and uses military force to maintain the Romani monopoly.

I suspect that you will agree that this situation would be tolerated only so long as the Muslim states were too weak to challenge Romani.

## *Israel's right to expansion*

This question is more easily resolved. The only defense of Israel's steady annexation of territory on the West Bank is that Arabs are implacably opposed to Israel's existence anyway, so that nothing is lost by Israel taking the arable land that is attractive for settlement.

The map shows Israeli settlements as of mid-2009. The dark line is the wall Israel is constructing and dark territory the settlements behind the wall. Settlements beyond the wall are black "dots" surrounded by white. The existence of a settlement does not mean a nearby city is settler dominated. For example, despite the proximity of settlements, there are only 500 Jewish residents in Hebron and none in Nablus. Nine percent of the West bank is settler occupied territory within the wall, eight percent of the West Bank is settler occupied territory beyond the wall. Note that the settlement area beyond the wall almost equals that within it. Together they total 17 percent. Things move quickly. Today (mid-2011) the total is closer to 20 percent.

The huge white area in the far East is the Jordan valley. It is Israeli controlled and 28.5 percent of the territory, but presumably would be part of a Palestinian state. Much of what remains for the Palestinians lacks water or is not suitable for cultivation.

Whatever their rhetoric every Israeli government has either tolerated or actively promoted expansion of the settlements. Sometimes plans to build more housing here or there are made public, but much expansion is hidden. While writing the original draft of this chapter, I received an email.

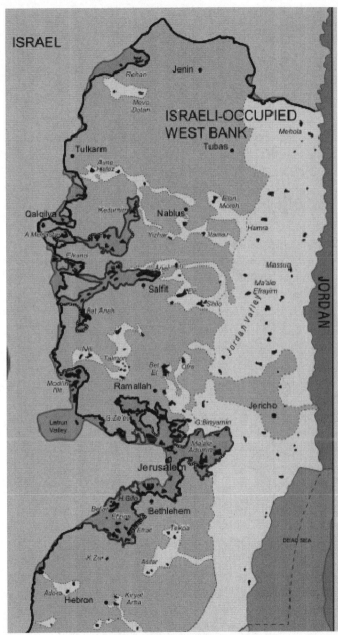

**Map 2. Settlements on the West Bank**

Source: PLO Mission to the United States (2009).

In South Hebron on the West Bank, a group of settlers are using a well recently appropriated from its Palestinian owner. They have got it classified as a "military zone" and now, protected by troops, they have exclusive use of it and its "former" owner is barred (if anyone wants exact names and places, email me).

Even moderate Arab opinion can never accept such a policy. The fact that the US either will not or cannot alter it makes every anti-Israeli Arab an anti-American Arab. No populist politician will fail to appeal to the sentiments aroused. Sometimes Americans are shocked by their rhetoric. But just as Southern orators once ranted about blacks and told lies (every black man a potential rapist), and right-wing orators today rant about socialism and tell lies (medical insurance marks the end of a free nation), so Arab orators will rant about Israel and tells lies (deny the Holocaust). Politicians behave like politicians no matter where you find them.

The Islamic people of the Middle East are enraged every time they hear America speak as if she regards the non-proliferation treaty as a sacred document. They do not see the case of Israel as some kind of innocent exception. They see Israel as she is: a power using its military dominance to pursue territorial expansion. They must try to match her strength in terms of conventional weapons, but are well aware that Israel will threaten to use nuclear weapons to reverse any victory they might achieve. Therefore, they must acquire their own nuclear weapons.

### The tide of history

The modernization of the Middle East is inevitable (see Box 11). Nation after nation will become sufficiently unified and acquire sufficient economic resources to achieve a nuclear capacity. The US seems to think that bringing popular government and economic progress to the Middle East will create nations with the psychology of cost accountants too busy making money to be anti-Israeli and anti-American. In fact, these historical trends will mean a steady supply of "rogue states" bent on nuclear parity with Israel.

---

### Box 11: Arabs and Irish

Islamic fundamentalists can delay this process but they will lose. Too many young people are going to the West and seeing what the modern world can offer. If the day when the Arab Middle East can match Israel is 30 or 50 years distant, will not animosity toward Israel simply fade way even if she has absorbed the West bank?

The author being Irish-American knows that it will not. Ireland got effective independence in 1922. In 1950, there were still Irish-Americans, men whose last Irish ancestor was one grandparent, wearing BFI (Bullets for Ireland) buttons. My cousin Jack had a small cannon in his back yard out of which he could fire beer cans filled with concrete. Even those who cannot fight on the front lines can do something.

---

I speak as if this lies in the future but events began to unfold over 30 years ago. In the late 1970s, Iraq purchased a nuclear reactor. In 1981, Israel became convinced they would use it to produce plutonium, and destroyed it with an air strike (Vandenbroucke,1984). By then, Iraq had attacked Iran precipitating a war that lasted until 1988. There was a history of border disputes, but an important motive was the fact that the Iranian revolution had brought a fundamentalist Shiite group to power. In Iraq, Sunni Moslems oppressed a larger group of Shiites, and they feared that Iran would foment a Shiite rebellion. President Reagan gave Saddam roughly $40 billion to fight Iran and more billions to keep him from turning to the USSR (Friedman, 1993).

Iraq resurrected her nuclear weapons program and began a biological weapons program. By 1984, she was using poison gas with great effectiveness against Iranian "human wave" attacks. The American CIA provided intelligence that was used by the Iraqis to target their chemical weapons strikes. On 21 March 1986, the United Nation Security Council recognized that "chemical weapons on many occasions have been used by Iraqi forces against Iranian forces". The United States cast the only dissenting vote. On 23 March 1988, Iraq used chemical weapons against Iranian troops and their Kurdish allies who held the town of Halabja. About 6,800 died, mostly Kurdish civilians. The Reagan administration nullified an attempt by Congress to cut off US assistance to Iraq as "premature", and accepted Iraq's preposterous claim that the Iranians were responsible. Oddly the Iranians still hold a grudge toward America and want a deterrent against hostile nations (Hiltermann, 2003).

In 1990, Iraq attacked Kuwait. This was supported by all Iraqi nationalists, whether Sunni or Shiite, who consider Kuwait a province of Iraq that had been alienated. America defeated Iraq in the Gulf War and afterwards, Iraq submitted to inspection (with varying degrees of obstruction). The UN found and destroyed much of her biological and nuclear warfare capacity. By then, the US had begun bombing targets in Iraq, partially to keep her army away from the Kurds, and led a UN embargo that was unusually effective in isolating Iraq and which lasted right up to the day of the US invasion on March 19, 2003.

A word about Syria: there is no doubt that Syria wants a nuclear capability. At present, she has only one small research reactor, but she has approached China, Russia, Iran, and North Korea for help in developing her nuclear program. In September of 2007, Israel bombed Al-Kibar. Both Israel and America claimed that it harbored an undeclared plutonium production reactor (Mazzetti and Cooper, 2007). At present, Syria has a weak industrial infrastructure, poor scientific capabilities, and lacks the trained engineers and other personnel needed to run a major civilian or weapons-oriented program. It is unlikely that she can acquire nuclear weapons in the near future.

Iran is the current candidate for an air strike. Over 100,000 Iranian troops and civilians died from Iraqi chemical weapons. Its supreme leader (Ali Khamenei) has issued a categorical decree against development, production, and use of nuclear weapons. Iran claims its uranium enrichment program is exclusively for peaceful purposes. Israel and the US suspect her intentions and estimate that she could attain nuclear capacity within three to five years. They emphasize her reluctance to submit to full inspection. Fitzpatrick (2008) gives a good overall view of nuclear programs in the Middle East in general and Iran in particular.

## Forbidding the tide to come in

Although a Catholic prelate, Cardinal Richelieu was a French nationalist. When Germany was divided into many small states, rather than favoring the Catholic faction, he tried to keep the Germans as weak and divided as possible. If you posit no rapprochement ever between Israel and Arabs, Israel's national interest is clear: welcome anything that impedes the unity and economic development of Arab states in the Middle East. Otherwise they may develop the air defenses, delivery systems, and nuclear weapons that would nullify your nuclear monopoly. This means periodic air raids such as that against Iraq in 1981 and Syria in 2007.

## Israel and America

Better if they fight one another as Iraq and Iran did setting back economic development in those nations by at least a decade. One unfortunate effect of overthrowing Sunni rule in Iraq is that now both she and Iran are ruled by Shiites and less likely to fight again. Better still, if America, in defiance of all her interests, can be got to do the job for you. Israel on her own could never have devastated Iraq to the degree America did by twelve years of bombing plus an invasion that has set her back at least another decade. Best of all, if you can get the US to bomb Iran.

As for America, the very association with Israel is destructive of her interests, particularly since Israel puts expansion into the West Bank ahead of conciliation with her Arab neighbors. This alone forbids America the role of a neutral arbiter that can be trusted to license nuclear weapons, and contribute to the pacification of the Middle East.

She is like an authority that has licensed only one person to carry a gun in a neighborhood saturated with mutual hatred. America not only refuses to face this, but a group called neo-cons (neo-conservatives) have become influential. They labor under the delusion that the nations of the Middle East have no sociology or history and are infinitely malleable and ready for "regime change". All America need do is send in an army, overthrow the existing government, collect some local sympathizers, read them the US Constitution, give them a lecture on the glory of the free market, provide some economic and technical aid, and history will flow towards a prosperous, democratic, contented, pro-American Middle East, tolerant of Israel.

## Who was Saddam Hussein?

Saddam Hussein was not a threat to anyone but his neighbors. He never aspired to do anything but make Iraq the dominant Arab state in his area, which is to say to become the major player a minor league. Iran taught him he could not even achieve that. He still aspired to be the hero of the Arab world, someone who could face down Israel some day, which meant he would eventually need a nuclear capacity. In the meantime, he supported terrorist activity against Israel, but in regard to al-Qaeda, the international terrorist network that threatens America, he was the best ally the US could have. The fundamentalists hated him as a secular ruler and he hunted them down religiously.

## Box 12: Saddam Hussein

Saddam Hussein was in effective control of Iraq by 1970. The population of Iraq is split into 20 percent Sunni Arabs, 60 percent Shiite Arabs, about 17 percent Kurds, and the other 3 percent are mainly Turkmen. Like all previous rulers, he was a Sunni, and tried to hold his nation together by a combination of oppression and economic development, much of it targeted at winning support among the other ethnic groups. The 1970s were his golden era. He used oil money to eliminate illiteracy and provide free schooling and health, agricultural development combined with land reform, good roads, and near universal electrification. Women enjoyed unprecedented freedoms and filled high-level government and industry jobs. UNESCO gave him an award.

In 1979, he conducted a bloody purge within his own party to ensure personal loyalty, and began to promote a cult of personality accompanied by the building of lavish palaces. In 1980, he attacked Iran. His use of gas against Iran (and an Iranian occupied Kurdish village) was with US collusion, whose fear that fundamentalist Iran might overwhelm Iraq almost equaled his own. His lost wars against Iran and Kuwait and the sanctions that followed undermined the prosperity of Iraq, increased the prospect of rebellion, and led to increased reliance on oppression, sometimes quite ruthless. Minority dictators need to kill more than those who represent an ethic majority.

He wrote novels about medieval romance, an Iraqi war hero who marries a Kurdish girl, the rise of his political party, and a Zionist-Christian conspiracy. He had no problem lining up a publisher. The CIA claims that at least the first novel was written with the help of a ghost writer (well they would).

The only al-Qaeda that operated on Iraq's territory was a small group in a remote area he could not reach, and they were dedicated to overthrowing his regime (Bergen, 2006).

Much has been made of the fact that after the invasion of Iraq, no hidden weapons of mass destruction were found. That is not my grievance. If ever a ruler put his head in the noose, it was Saddam Hussein. Having nothing to hide, he should have pleaded for inspectors and aided them in every way, rather than behaving like he had something to hide. My point is that whether he was developing such weapons was irrelevant to whether the US should try to replace him.

Everyone got sucked into a pseudo-debate. The notion that a nuclear Iraq would threaten Europe or America with missiles was absurd. America deterred the might of Joseph Stalin and the USSR for over 40 years, and we are to believe she could not deter a pipsqueak dictator in the Middle East. In order to make him appear as a menace to the US, rather than merely to Israel, Saddam had to be portrayed as a madman beyond the bounds of reason, with a compulsive desire for personal and national suicide, beyond restraint from any other actor even inside his own nation. Needless to say, reality and the portrait had little in common (see Box 12).

The same propaganda is now circulating with regard to the Mahmoud Ahmadinejad, the President of Iran, who does not even have authority over foreign and military policy. He is subordinate to Ayatollah Khamenei, the Supreme Leader. He can sign treaties with other countries and international organizations and appoint ambassadors (subject to the approval of the parliament). But control over foreign policy and the armed forces, including the nuclear policy of the Iranian state, are the prerogatives of the Supreme Leader. The Supreme Leader even has effective power to determine who will be allowed to stand for President.

I do not doubt that Saddam wanted weapons of mass destruction, and suspect that their absence merely showed he had learned something. It is no good trying to build nuclear weapons until you have the air defenses needed to deter Israeli bombing, and ideally delivery systems that can penetrate Israeli defenses. His weapons program from 1990 to 2003, as in 1981, was an Israeli problem. If Israel had chosen to attack him again, the Iraq affair would have been just another bombing episode along the road of Israel's struggle against the modernization of the Middle East. American's probity would not have been compromised in the eyes of nations like Russia, Germany, and France.

All of America's interests screamed to leave Saddam for Israel to deal with as she would. And yet, what began as a hope of overthrowing his regime in 1990 hardened into a resolve by 2003. I can only assume that the US invaded Iraq because she took the nation-building scenario of the neo-cons seriously. I doubt it was oil. If so, America reads history very badly. Oil producing nations like to maximize profits and if the US can bid competitively, she will get her share. The only chance her bids will be rejected on political grounds is posed by her present policy, namely, her association with an Israel unwilling to create a viable Palestinian state. For those of you who are thinking "Israel cannot do that on her own", hold your objections until the latter part of this chapter.

## *Educating Israel*

If Israel had found that it strained her resources to deal with Saddam, that would have been salutary. Let us hope that it taxes her resources to bomb Iran. Israel must face the fact that one day it will be beyond her capacity to intimidate the entire Middle East. Sooner or later modernization will bring a manifesto by three or four (who knows who will rule Pakistan by then) Middle East nations to this effect: "Israel must admit that she has these weapons and dismantle them within a year with the inspection so dear to your hearts. Or all four of us will go nuclear as fast as we can. Invade us if you will, and see if you can subdue the lands from the Aegean Sea to India and recreate the empire of Alexander the Great. Let Israel bomb us all if she dares. We now have the air defenses to make that very costly."

## Moral questions

America should not have used sanctions against Iraq between 1990 and 2003 or invaded Iraq in 2003. The former is more damning than the latter. By using sanctions, the US set a *goal* destructive of human life with full awareness of the consequences. The invasion killed many but, thanks to political blindness, these qualify as *unforeseen consequences*.

### The sanctions

The sanctions included bombing, no fly zones (areas in which Iraqi planes were not to operate), freezing all of Iraq's oversea assets, and an embargo on both imports and exports including oil. Even air flights to and from Iraq were banned. Iraq was allowed to import goods for humanitarian purposes, but without her overseas assets and oil revenue, she had no money to pay for them. The embargo was never totally effective thanks to smuggling, and some Arab states made good money from illegal trade in oil. In December 1996, the oil for food program relaxed the strictures somewhat, when a limited amount of oil revenue was made available to trade for food and medicines.

On 26 March 1997, America made public the fact that she wished sanctions to remain in place until Saddam Hussein was overthrown. In her first major foreign policy address, Secretary of State Madeleine Albright said : "Iraq must prove its peaceful intentions" and that "the evidence is overwhelming that Saddam Hussein's intentions will never be peaceful" (Wallensteen, Staibano, & Eriksson, 2003).

### How many people did the sanctions kill?

There is no doubt that by hindering oil exports, her major source of income, the sanctions were disastrous for the Iraqi economy and welfare state, particularly since Iraq was trying to recover from the impact of two wars.

An initial UN report caused a sensation by putting the rise in mortality at 500,000, mostly children, and many attributed all of these deaths to the sanctions (the UN later revised its estimates downward). Richard Garfield of Columbia University, a competent epidemiologist, provided a better analysis. He concluded that between August 1991 and March 1998, there were at least 106,000 excess deaths of children under 5, with a "more likely" worst-case sum of 227,000. Not long before the invasion ended sanctions, he updated the latter figure to 350,000, noting that the rate had tailed off after 1996 (the oil for food program). He said that only a portion of the excess deaths were due to sanctions, the remainder being caused by the devastating effects on Iraq of her lost wars (Garfield, 1999).

Matt Welch was an editor at the *Los Angeles Times* and now edits *Reason Magazine*, an excellent libertarian journal. When the staff of the daily features section of the *Chicago Tribune* ranked all magazines in America, they put it at 13. Citing Garfield's early 1998 estimate, Welch attributed at least 100,000 deaths to sanctions, which is 40 percent of the "more likely" excess death total. This suggests more than 125,000 deaths by the end of sanctions (Welch, 2002).

Garfield was never rash enough to commit himself to an exact "sanctions caused" figure. But as of 1998, he did say "there have been many more sanctions-related deaths than deaths resulting from the Gulf War" (Garfield, 1999). The Project on Defense Alternatives study puts the latter at about 27,000 of which about 86 percent were military dead (Conetta, 2003). If many more means four times as many, we get 100,000 + 25,000 (after early 1998) or 125,000. I will let this stand as a reasonable if conservative estimate.

## Moral judgment on sanctions

In 1996, the institution of the oil for food program partially alleviated the situation. The new program did not satisfy everyone. In 1998, the UN humanitarian coordinator for Iraq, Denis Halliday, ended a 34-year career with the UN.

He resigned and traveled around the world calling the policy "genocide". His replacement, Hans von Sponeck, also resigned in protest as did Jutta Burghardt, head of the World Food Program in Iraq (Welch, 2002). Whatever good relaxed sanctions did, no credit goes to the United States. It was not America that caused the UN to relent, but a huge outcry over the tally (exaggerated) of dead children.

America's attitude was expressed by Secretary of State Albright in an interview on 12 May 1996 on the *60 Minutes* program. Lesley Stahl asked her, "We have heard that half a million children have died. . . . is the price worth it?" Albright replied, "We think the price is worth it". Later in her autobiography, she said that she had answered a loaded question. She should have disputed the exaggerated estimate and explained Saddam's culpability (Albright, 2003).

This raises three points: (1) What made the deaths worth it, of course, was the hope that sanctions would overthrow Saddam. *Reply:* this could occur only by inflicting great misery on the Iraqi people, which makes that an intended goal. (2) Could Saddam have mitigated or eliminated suffering through humane behavior? *Reply:* he could have mitigated the suffering somewhat, but since that was not a reasonable expectation, it does nothing to exonerate the sanctions. (3) The 500,000 figure was a gross exaggeration. *Reply:* True, but 125,000 innocent deaths is quite enough to make the policy immoral.

The goal of removing Saddam is utterly damning because it entails that the means of removing him was your proximate goal. Just as removing the Vietnamese backed regime in Cambodia necessitated a conscious policy of supporting Pol Pot, so the objective of overthrowing Saddam necessitated a conscious policy of inflicting the misery that was to do the job.

At one time, I hoped that US policy makers had suppressed from consciousness the detail of just how sanctions would affect Iraq and its children. But then,

Professor Thomas Nagy (2001) of the School of Business and Public Management at George Washington University revealed the contents of declassified documents of the Defense Intelligence Agency (DIA).

Should the reader doubt what follows, see Hassan (2004) for their location on the internet. I could hardly bear to read them. **Disease Outbreaks in Iraq**: "The most likely diseases during next 60–90 days (in descending order), Diarrhea diseases (particularly children), Acute respiratory illnesses (colds and influenza), Typhoid, Hepatitis A (particularly children), Measles, diphtheria, and pertussis (particularly children), Meningitis, including meningococcal (particularly children), Cholera (possible, but less likely)." **Iraq Water Treatment Vulnerabilities** (dated January 22, 1991): "With no domestic sources of both water treatment replacement parts and some essential chemicals, *Iraq will continue attempts to circumvent UN sanctions to import these vital commodities* (italics added). Failing to secure supplies will result in a shortage of pure drinking water for much of the population. This could lead to increased incidences, if not epidemics, of disease".

As the italics show, the US knew that sanctions would do harm. When America could, she tried to maximize the harm. In early 2001, she withheld $280 million in medical supplies on the grounds that the vaccines included live cultures that could be used for biological warfare (Gordon, 2002).

As for the contention that Saddam might have mitigated the effects of the sanction were he more humane, this does nothing to mitigate the immorality of US policy. Assume that Pol Pot had regained power. The fact that he, rather than his Chinese and American backers, killed the first 125,000 Cambodians would have been no excuse: because that behavior was predictable. Even if Saddam's lack of humanity, rather than the sanctions alone, contributed to the deaths of 125,000 Iraqi children, that was no excuse: that behavior was predictable.

If Saddam had been a model of humanity, there would (we hope) have been no sanctions. There were sanctions precisely because he was not that kind of person. America knew, absolutely knew, that its policy would mean the suffering of innocents. And the more the better. If you know that an alcoholic beats his children when drunk, and give him a bottle, you are not innocent of what follows. There is only one historical example of innocent sanctions altering the behavior of a regime. Thanks to its obsession with rugby, a rugby boycott, incredible as it seems, may have helped end Apartheid in South Africa. It is a pity that Iraq was not obsessed with cricket.

I do not accept that Saddam's want of humanity was the primary cause of why the sanctions bit. Saddam did use some of his resources (after sanctions) to indulge whims like presidential palaces. But that did not cost real money. He does not appear to have salted billions away either at home or abroad. After the invasion, the assets of his family and closest associates were frozen and there were high expectations of seizing large sums of money. However, efforts to locate the money were surprisingly unsuccessful (Wallensteen, Staibano, & Eriksson, 2003).

The notion that Saddam ignored the suffering of children because of sadism is absurd. Recall that in happier times he established a welfare state that provided universal and free education and health care. A large slice of post-sanctions funds that could have been used for welfare was diverted to please the army and keep his political entourage happy. This is only to say he did not wish to commit suicide. A despot had better keep his army and potential rivals happy. Plato as usual diagnosed the situation. The tyrant is like a slave-owner on an island surrounded by his slaves. He had better have a "loyal" army and supporters. What did America expect? When resources are short, men with guns in their hands are the last to suffer.

Two points have been offered by way of rebuttal. First, that sanctions against other nations, such as Libya and

Yugoslavia, did not impact on child health to the degree they did in Iraq. This ignores that Iraq was different. Iraq was heavily dependent on oil revenue and was already crippled by war. The sanctions against her were much more comprehensive, multilateral, and imposed virtually overnight so no ameliorative measures could be taken. As Garfield (1999) says, embargoes under these conditions maximize the impact on the health of the general population.

Second, there was an autonomous region in the Kurdish north where relief was controlled by the UN rather than Saddam. UNICEF (1999) compared child mortality in two periods: 1984 to 1989, war years, with 1994 to 1998, sanction years, the latter being weighted towards the period after sanctions had been ameliorated. They found that child mortality actually showed a slight decline in the north while more than doubling in the south. This was taken as evidence that Saddam's administration of the oil for food program was entirely responsible for child deaths in the areas under his control. The report itself makes no such claim. UNICEF Executive Director Carol Bellamy noted that after 1989, the north got large amounts of international aid not available to the south.

Arnove (2000) summarizes the differences between the north and south. Not only did the Kurdish north receive humanitarian assistance for a longer period, but it had better agriculture. It suffered much less from bombing. Evading sanctions was easier because its borders are far more porous. It received UN-controlled assistance in currency, while the rest of the country received only commodities. Finally, it simply got more aid. Arnove says that the south received 82 percent of the north's per capita aid from the oil-for-food program (100 divided by 122). I put the difference much higher. From 1996 to 1998, the north received 13 percent of the oil revenues and it contains 13 percent of the population. The south received 53 per cent to allocate among 87 percent of the population (the rest of the money went for expenses and a Kuwaiti relief fund). That puts aid to the south at only

61 percent of the north's per capita aid (53 divided by 87 = 0.61).

I have no doubt that UN administered aid in the north was better allocated than Saddam administered aid in the South. But the difference has clearly been exaggerated. More to the point, it does not affect the moral equation.

## The war in Iraq

The US invaded Iraq in March of 2003. As of June 2006, *The Lancet* put the death toll at 600,000 (Burnham, Lafta, Doocy, & Roberts, 2006). Accepting that estimate suggests that the present total is about one million. There is much debate about *The Lancet's* estimate, but in my mind the debate has been settled by the current Iraqi government. On 21 January 2008, the Ministry of Labor and Social Affairs released a report estimating that there were 4.5 million Iraqi orphans (MHRI, 2008). Two months earlier, a press conference attended by the Minister of Human Rights, put the figure at 5 million (Hussein, 2007). Since these reports are now three years out of date, I will take 5 million as approximately correct. That is 35 percent of Iraq's children.

You do not have orphans without dead parents. Can less than a million parents have died violently (other than from natural causes)? Some adults who were not parents were also killed. Almost half of the Iraqi population is 18 or below. So if over a million adults have died, hundreds of thousands of children have died, children who did not live to become orphans. Orphans include only those under the age of 18, so they must all have been orphaned since 1990. By that year, Iraq's earlier wars had ended. A million deaths seems a modest estimate.

## Moral judgment on the war

After World War I, the British imposed a Hāshimite monarchy on Iraq, which is say Sunni dominance, even though Sunni were only 20 percent of the population.

During the British occupation, the Shiites and Kurds fought for independence (Sluglett, 2008).

In 2003, the overthrow of 85 years of Sunni hegemony by Shiites was going to cause bloodshed. There slowly evolved what amounted to a civil war with ethnic expulsion. Shiite-led Iraqi government troops and Shiite militias fought against Sunnis. They won the bitter battle for Baghdad in 2006 to 2007, and partitioned the capitol in their favor. They now control three-quarters of Baghdad and Sunni fear death if they return to what were once their homes. Many of those who could fled the country. Al Qaeda, previously absent in Iraq, did as much as they could to make mischief but as ethnic conflict declined, they had no fire to fuel (Cockburn, 2008).

From January to May 2007, Bush launched a troop surge of US forces into Iraq, and by the year's end the level of violence fell. Some say the troops were the extra forces needed to pacify Baghdad and other trouble spots. Others argue that the worst of the civil war was over by mid-2007, with Baghdad and the nation effectively partitioned between Shiite and Sunni, and that the US finally had the sense to reassure Sunni that they were not to be massacred. US personnel on the spot gave them a lot of money, some of which could be spent on arms, which they found reassuring. Tens of thousands of Sunni tribesmen agreed to stop fighting when they were absorbed into the police and went on the payroll. I doubt anyone knows how to weight the factors involved (Feldman, 2008).

What concerns me is the many killed in the civil war while it lasted. The fact that America did not anticipate this bloodshed is less excusable than the fact that she did not anticipate the extra deaths her intervention in Vietnam entailed. To regime-build in a nation you have not bothered to learn anything about is a affront to practical wisdom. But once again, however necessary it was to oppose a policy in which obtuseness led to horrific consequences, and however disillusioning it is to realize that America has twice embarked on such ventures, it is not as troubling as her other policies. I refer to those that have had human suffering as either a conscious high risk (Pol Pot) or a conscious goal (the sanctions).

Has anything good come of the Iraq war? I suspect there has been one solid gain. When a 20 percent minority subordinates a 60 percent majority, they must be much more repressive than when the reverse is true. Iraq may have been the one Middle Eastern country in which outside military intervention greased the wheels of history. Sunni dominance was not going to last forever and whenever it was overthrown, there was going to be a civil war with many dead.

But it was not up to America to dictate when Iraq would get one million of her people killed and one-third of her children orphaned. Iraq has a population of 30 million of whom 14 million are children. It is as if someone had done America the favor of provoking a civil war that killed 10 million people and created 25 million orphans. Even if the toll were one-half or one third of my estimate, this ethnic struggle should have been left to the Iraqis to resolve.

### The first behavioral analysis

I have implied that the behavior of Israel and America is irrational and argued that America's actions are to be condemned. Such behavior cries out for explanation. Clearly, these nations are influenced by factors other than their national interests. Elsewhere I have distilled three factors from current international relations theory: national interest, perceived affinities and antagonisms with other nations, and identity. Here, I will use the spectacles these concepts afford to try to understand Israeli and then American policy.

*Israel through the spectacles*

- *National Interest:* Maximize Israel's chances of survival

- *Identity:* Savior of Jewish people and their culture; a minority believe they are God's chosen people with a mandate to restore Israel's biblical boundaries
- *Natural allies:* America
- *Natural enemies:* the Islamic world, particularly the Middle East

## Israel's identity

Some of the reasons that obscure Israeli thinking about her interests apply to all states. Both Israel and the Arabs feel that they win the blaming game, the game of saying who did what to whom and who was most wicked. There is also the primitive nationalism that delights in annexing more and more land. Other factors reflect Israel's national identity.

Many orthodox Jews believe that the West Bank belongs to Israel by Divine command, and rush in to settle no matter whether the government actively aids them or simulates a feeble opposition. Many non-orthodox Israelis have a romantic image of the settlers. In the early days, all Jews admired settlers as heroic people morally superior to themselves. They were the frontiersmen of Zionism, sharing hardship and reward with an equality to which we all pay lip service, and with the Calvinist virtues of hard work and frugality that Americanized Jews admired. Even Jewish atheists acknowledge a debt to the Orthodox. It was they who preserved Jewish identity throughout centuries of dispersal and persecution.

## Recent history

From 1948 (the war of independence) to 1967 (the Six-Day War), Israel did what any other nascent state would have done. The war of independence was a fight for survival. Both sides aimed at ethnic clearing (I do not use "cleansing" because of its emotive overtones). The Arabs wanted to expel the Jews; the Jews wanted to displace as many Arabs as they could and expand Israel's boundaries. Both sides sometimes massacred the other. The Jews won the battles and therefore the clearing contest (Esber, 2009; Morris, 2008).

In 1949, Israel began building a nuclear reactor and reprocessing plant. By 1969, she had nuclear weapons, technically financed by Jewish donors abroad, but her overall arms program and economy was supported by huge US contributions. In the 1970s, she conducted nuclear tests in conjunction with South Africa and by 2008, possessed between at least 200 nuclear warheads and the ability to deliver them by land, sea, and air (Feldman & Shapir, 2004; NTI, 2010).

In the 1967 war, Israel acquired territory on the West Bank of the Jordan River and control over all of Jerusalem. The Israeli Cabinet saw that Jewish settlements on the West Bank might undermine her long-term security and debated whether to bar them. Sadly, religious political parties hold the balance of power in Israeli politics and settlement proceeded. In late 2008, Prime Minister Olmert, shortly to leave office, stated that Israel would never secure peace with her Arab neighbors unless she helped create a viable Palestinian state, which included virtually the whole West Bank and some portion of East Jerusalem (Bronner, 2008).

## Giving away the West Bank

Even Olmert did not shed the mindset of the statesman. He wanted treaties to guarantee peace, pieces of paper signed by someone. The only way to give away the West Bank is to just do it. Israel could simply make a declaration tomorrow to the effect that: the Palestinian authorities will henceforth approve or deny all new housing starts on the West Bank and in Arab neighborhoods in Jerusalem; that she accepts that these territories constitute a Palestinian state; and that the long-term future of the Jewish settlements is that they will be fully integrated into that state.

This declaration should be followed with a tentative scenario:

(1) Israeli settlements will have, for now, a local administration protected by Israeli arms and under Israeli courts.

(2) Those presently in the settlements will have dual citizenship and constitute the sole legal Jewish residents on the West Bank. Visitors will have limited visas. New residents will be confined to those few who can make a case on compassionate grounds. Presumably they can be accommodated without new housing, and any new edifice not approved by the Palestinian authority will be pulled down. Legal residents will have a card that must be shown on many occasions. The penalty for illegal residence is deportation to Israel and 5 years in prison.

(3) Legal residents with dual citizenship need not serve in the Palestinian armed forces. But aside from local elections, they can vote only in Palestinian elections. Aside from local levies, they will pay the taxes the Palestinian authority sets for is citizens. Israeli officials would collect and transmit the revenue. They will travel on a Palestinian passport.

(4) Dual citizens who wish to relocate to Israel will receive generous assistance. They must sell all residential property they own to the Israeli government at market value. The Israeli government will resell these dwellings to Palestinians only.

(5) By agreement between Israel and Palestine, a small but steady flow of Palestinians would move into the settlements. If and when they became a majority, they would dominate the local administration and take over the police and courts.

(6) Israel reserves the right to take military action against anyone who attacks either Israel proper or her citizens on the West Bank.

The virtue of the unilateral "peace treaty" I have proposed is that it requires no immediate cooperation from Palestinians. If the Palestinian Authority refuses to issue new building permits, a moratorium for a few years will do no harm. If they issue no residence cards, Israel issues them. If they won't take the tax revenue, put it in a Swiss bank and send them the passbook. The "treaty" would demonstrate that Israel no longer intends to use the excuse that no Arab leader can give her peace to absorb as much of the West Bank as she can.

## Israeli politics

When I discuss such a plan with Israelis, I get a curious response. They say that a majority of Israeli citizens might well be persuaded; but that the religious parties hold the balance of power and that any government that was favorable would be brought down.

If the majority really were persuaded, the political problem could be solved. Certainly the survival of Israel takes precedence over normal politics. The leaders of the secular parties would be emboldened to go to the electorate with the idea of a grand coalition. They would compromise other issues for the time being and isolate the religious parties, and any who care to side with them, on the opposition benches. Or they might fall back on a more modest expedient that would have to be adopted anyway sooner or later (you cannot shelve politics as usual forever). You have a series of minority secular governments kept in power because the chief opposition party will vote with them on budget and supply for an agreed period. In other words, you just treat those elected by the religious parties as if they did not exist. Any party that can forge a coalition with a majority among non-religious members of parliament is treated as if it had an absolute majority.

This of course is nothing new. It has been used to isolate a party (say a racist or neo-fascist party) so that it cannot influence mainstream politics. But it is dependent on public perception that any minority group that vetoes Israel's best chance of survival is a menace to the body politic.

## The peace dividend

Every Israeli wants the impossible: they want the violence to stop now. The evacuation of the Gaza strip was a great trauma. Rather than a peace dividend Israeli got an even more hostile government next door. Now they say, why should giving up the West Bank be any different? It will not be different.

The immediate result of a genuine step toward peace is the savage reaction of those opposed to peace. No matter what she does, Israel may suffer acts of terrorism for the next 100 years. Spain does not have peace from the attacks of separatist fanatics. There may always be a splinter group of the Irish Republican Army that gives Britain no peace. No Arab leader can control all of the fanatics. What you get from signing over the West bank is not a peace dividend but an image dividend. And it may, just may, give you tolerable rather than intolerable violence in the long run. It is your only long-term hope of isolating the fanatic from the moderate. The slogan "trading land for peace" is utterly mischievous. It should be "giving away land for hope".

## The peace negotiations

The absurd "peace negotiations" are an escape from reality. A real treaty would put the head of an Arab leader in a noose. He would have to agree to forfeit the right of return, that is, the right of displaced Palestinians to repossess land in what is now Israel proper. Rabin was assassinated because of his moderate views and I believe Arafat would have been assassinated had he agreed to anything minimally acceptable to Israel.

The American media should stop the charade of sober comment on the latest negotiation, the latest US diplomat wandering around the Middle East to encourage "dialogue", and simply tell the truth: at present neither side can publically agree on what could be done to avoid a perennial conflict. All treaties can do is to add a new dimension to the blaming game: accusations about who has not kept their word about what.

## The shadow of the holocaust

It is impossible to find a historical analogy to the interaction between America as patron and Israel as client state. Israeli Prime Ministers humiliate American Presidents with regularity. A President "urges" a halt to the expansion of the settlements. The next day, an Israeli spokesman says that Israel has no intention of halting construction. Whoever heard of a client state that felt free to treat its patron with such contempt? There is a sharp contrast between Israeli behavior and that of America's other client state Taiwan. Taiwan's leaders may think of non-Chinese as barbarians, but they have never defied the US so openly.

Why does Israel go out of its way to gratuitously insult America? I suspect that it is because of the shadow of the Holocaust. Western nations closed their borders to Jews trying to escape Hitler. Who have the Jews ever been able to trust but themselves? Think of the psychological price of a conscious admission that Israel's future is dependent on the good will of a gentile state. Think of the need to prove that Israel is self-sufficient, that she can afford to defy her patron, even though such defiance verges on the suicidal. A Jewish scholar tells me this omits something about Jewish identity: their history has made them hate taking orders from anyone.

### The second behavioral analysis

If anything, American behavior is more baffling than that of Israel. At least, if you assume that no rapprochement between Israel and her Arab neighbors is possible, what Israel does makes sense. The fact that America has never disassociated herself from Israel, has not even made an honest effort to deter Israel's expansionist policies, makes no sense at all. I will again use the three-factor spectacles and see what they can do.

## America and Israel

- *National interest:* How to reconcile the tension between two policy goals: the preservation of Israel and the pacification of the Middle East
- *Identity:* American exceptionalism, that is, America untainted by the vices of the old world
- *Natural allies:* Europe and Australasia by cultural affinity; Japan with reservoir of good will from the occupation and as a protectorate; Israel by cultural affinity and as a protectorate; Taiwan as a protectorate
- *Natural enemies:* Latin America due to history of intervention; the Middle East, due to history of intervention and the US commitment to Israel
- *Ambiguous:* India and Pakistan because America vacillates between them; Russia due to recent great power rivalry; China because of US support of Taiwan with the complication of economic interdependence; Sub-Sahara Africa due to the status of black America but impressed by election of Obama

## American support for Israel

Partly, this is because of the American political system. The method of electing a President is that each state has electoral votes roughly in accord with its population, and these votes are awarded on the principle of winner takes all. US voters are about evenly divided between the two major parties, so it is vital to win big states like New York and Florida and get their large blocs of electoral votes. Also campaigns are expensive to finance. Jewish Americans are concentrated in these states and do much to subsidize campaigns.

However, this would mean little if sympathy did not run deep. As for people in general, the Bible permeates the American consciousness. That creates a presumption that the land of Israel in some sense belongs to the Jewish people. More important is the relationship of affection and mutual respect between US intellectuals and American Jews, one that for its intensity is historically unique. Non-Jewish intellectuals marry Jews, have close friendships with Jews, interact with Jewish colleagues, and know how much poorer the US cultural scene would be without them. They have friendships with other minorities of course, but these are not minorities whose history of persecution is so manifest, whose very existence was recently threatened by a lunatic, whose whole history and identity is bound up with a foreign nation state. It becomes unthinkable to tell Jewish Americans that the state of Israel is at risk (see Box 13).

---

### Box 13: The state of Israel

Who would want the state of Israel to be at risk? No one who has read Amos Oz's memoir, *A tale of love and darkness* (Oz, 2003). Its creation is an incredible manifestation of the spirit of a people who refused to be crushed by dispersal, persecution, indifference, the limitations of a dead language, and a rocky soil. What has not been solved is how to preserve Israel without making its history a tragedy for its people, its neighbors, and America's potential to do good.

---

Foreign policy is unlike domestic policy. Other than when the American people find their children dying abroad in a pointless war, foreign policy is formulated by opinion elites, which is to say by American intellectuals. Explaining why America supports Israel at all is easy. Explaining why America is so oblivious to the price this entails is more difficult.

## American exceptionalism

Exceptionalism is the belief that your nation has virtues all others lack. Every nation suffers from this delusion but few are so far removed from reality as to be surprised if the rest of the world does not share its good opinion of itself. The founding fathers and many Europeans thought of America as a brave new world that would find a special moral purity because of its isolation from the wickedness of the old world. This is reflected in the writings of Jefferson and his contemporaries (Flynn, 2008, chapter 1).

The speeches of America's presidents from Wilson (make the world safe for democracy) to Roosevelt (the four freedoms) to Bush (the axis of evil) are like sermons from a kindly but indignant pastor to a congregation in need of instruction. They are just speeches but America really believes its speeches. Morgenthau (1948) relates two incidents. In 1918, at Versailles, a French diplomat asked a member of the American delegation when Wilson was going to stop making speeches "like a professor", and get down to the real business of bargaining over who was to get what when they redrew the map of Europe. In 1945, at Yalta, Churchill was alarmed when he realized that Roosevelt had no strategic sense of the need to counter Stalin's ambitions in Eastern Europe.

Once America had made up its mind that it was good to save Israel from extinction that was that. The fact that Israel was established by displacement of the local population, the fact that it has never respected reasonable limits to its expansion, the fact that it uses air strikes to enforce a nuclear monopoly in an area divided by hate, these are mere bagatelles. Israel is an American ally, its people have a place in American hearts, its government resembles American democracy. American, American, American—clearly to be American is to be something very special. America would of course prefer other nations to endorse its actions in the Middle East. That would speak well of them and would enhance America's strength.

However, whether they do or not has no effect on the moral equation: The US has the right to act unilaterally because its motives are pure. What is the matter with foreigners? Can they not recognize *goodness* when they see it? As Colin Powell said, wiping a tear from his eye: "Our history of the last 50, 60 years is quite clear. We have liberated a number of countries, and we do not own one square foot of any of those countries except where we bury our dead" (Lehrer, 2003).

Well, given all that, should a few million extra deaths because of ignorance and illusion count for much? After all, these are the sins of a child, and easily forgiven. But the rest of the world wants America to grow up. The world is getting nervous: they anticipate a new generation of weapons that will allow America to kill anyone, anywhere, without casualties (see Box 14).

---

**Box 14: The right of citizens to bear bees**

When bee-sized drones that kill anything that moves get cheap enough, will the National Rifleman's Association defend the right of Americans to possess them? Despite the right of citizens to bear arms, I predict they will lose this one. It is thus that a free people are stripped of their ancient liberties.

---

To put the matter in a sentence: America does not feel it *deserves* to pay a price for its support of Israel; therefore, no one *should* make it pay a price; therefore, if anyone does, that shows that they are simply *immoral*. Recall how America reacted to the opposition of Russia and France to the invasion of Iraq: they had financial interests in Iraq that they were cynically trying to protect. In contrast, Eastern Europe (the "new Europe") truly valued things like freedom. They saw America's mission for what it was, a crusade for freedom throughout the Middle East. Europeans have never understood just how much America's self image distorts its perception of political reality.

America's faith, that it can convince people to be good if it just shows them what goodness really is, has a certain charm. In *Time Magazine*, Joe Kline (2008) wrote sensibly about Afghanistan. He describes its divisions except when its people unite to "humiliate" a Western presence that outlasts its welcome, and he describes US involvement as an "aimless absurdity". What does he recommend? Telling the government in Kabul that they simply must stop being corrupt and shut down the drug trade — or else. No French journalist could write anything so odd. The presumption that the past and present will melt in the presence of moral fervor is as American as apple pie.

## What kind of commitment?

A delusion shared by many in both Israel and America is that an unconditional US commitment is the best guarantee of Israel's security. In fact, if Israel is allowed to act in a way that makes any reconciliation with her neighbors unlikely, the long-term price America pays for alienating the Arab world may become intolerable. Thus far, the price has been a few episodic events like the Twin Towers. But if the Arab states ever play the oil card, those of us who support Israel may find public tolerance does not extend to less money in people's pockets. There are already signs that American intellectuals are becoming more and more enraged because they are forbidden to even discuss the price America pays for its "ally".

American support of Israel should be absolute only in the sense that America's commitment to Japan and Iceland is absolute. They are treated as if they were part of American soil, with all of America's might as a deterrent to anyone who might threaten their existence. But American support should be conditional on the integration of the West Bank into a viable Palestinian state, and American aid to Israel contingent on her acceptance of that condition. Whatever Israel's response, America would reap an enormous and immediate dividend throughout the Islamic world.

America's present commitment is suspect precisely because it is unconditional. Israel has a choice between an unconditional commitment likely to expire and a conditional commitment likely to persist. Absolute security she will never get. That is not the stuff of politics.

## Pacification of the Middle East

Despite its policy failures and moral lapses, there is no doubt that America does want to pacify the Middle East. Its present policy is that the Middle East should be a nuclear free zone except for Israel. To state this policy is to make manifest its absurdity. True pacification of the Middle East must take place in four stages: Israel creates a viable Palestinian state on the West Bank inclusive of East Jerusalem; Arab states accept the existence of Israel within those borders; America extends her guarantee of territorial integrity beyond Israel to all Middle Eastern states that forgo weapons of mass destruction (and expansion of their borders by force); Israel now must meet this new condition, that is, to retain her American guarantee she too must become nuclear free.

Israel's nuclear monopoly will be broken. The only choice is whether several Middle East states shall have weapons of mass destruction, or whether none shall have them. The first alternative is the inevitable outcome of periodic Israeli bombing and episodic US invasions. The US must face up to political reality and give the second alternative a chance. And that entails a hard truth: her commitment to Israel must become conditional.

# Chapter 6

# *Obama through September 2011*

It is dangerous to speculate what Obama's administration will accomplish but I will hazard a few guesses about foreign policy. Obama is a highly intelligent man whose life history shows that he has other-regarding principles. As the first Black President, he will want to leave office with a verdict that he conducted himself with dignity and did nothing new that divided America. That implies that he will be reluctant to take radical steps, both those that are needed and those that would be mischievous. My guesses: no re-thinking of America's relationship with Israel and therefore, no real progress towards a nuclear-free Middle East or enforcement of the Nuclear Non-Proliferation Treaty; the prospect of getting US troops out of the Middle East and a strong reluctance to commit troops to that area again.

## Obama and Israel

In March 2010, in order to promote peace negotiations, Vice-President Joe Biden arrived in Israel. He was greeted with an announcement that Israel planned to build 1,600 new Jewish housing units in predominately-Arab East Jerusalem.

I think that the timing was an accident. Secretary of State Hillary Clinton phoned Prime Minister Netanyahu to express "frustration" (Kessler, 2010). The latter expressed regret over the timing of the announcement, but said that Jerusalem was Israel's and that housing there was entirely her affair. There was a "tense" meeting between Obama and Netanyahu at the White House. The Israeli newspaper *Haaretz* claimed that the US wants a four-month settlement freeze to induce the Palestinians to have direct talks with Israel. Leaks from the Obama administration say that even this may be negotiable. He may be open to the possibility that Netanyahu might suggest alternative ideas that would be "creative" (Rogin, 2010).

On 19 May 2011, Obama said that a Palestinian state should be based on the 1967 boundaries with "swaps", as if Israel is really willing to trade territory within her heartland sufficient to compensate for the major settlements on the West Bank (Landler & Myers, 2011). This tepid statement earned him a lecture by Netanyahu, and Obama emphasized that negotiations would leave some Israeli settlements intact. Does he see that the whole notion of a negotiated settlement is an illusion? If so, he has not told Joe Biden, the chief US negotiator, who continues to upbraid the Palestinians for setting pre-conditions to negotiations (Black & Milne, 2011).

As this book goes to press, the UN Security Council is considering whether to recognize the state of Palestine inclusive of the Gaza Strip, the whole West Bank, and East Jerusalem. America is trying to line up votes to defeat the proposal. Obama has said that, if necessary, the United States will cast a veto. So we now know the sad truth. Either Obama has not faced up to reality or believes he could not be re-elected if he acknowledged reality: that negotiations are futile; that Israel can create a viable Palestinian state at any time; that what might induce her to do so would be an announcement that he will veto legislation that authorizes aid to Israel; and that Israel's nuclear monopoly cannot persist. Israel has chosen this moment to announce 1100 new housing starts in East Jerusalem. Once again, she has made public her contempt for the United States and its interests.

## Obama and Afghanistan

Obama wants to end the Afghan war. It seems that all but the military have faced up to the limitations on what a Western army can accomplish in Afghanistan. But who knows what is to come? It is worth rehearsing the folly of those who believed in nation-building, that is, the notion that America could create a peaceful united nation with a democratic and corruption-free government.

The recent attempt by US and NATO forces to influence political events in Afghanistan is the fifth foreign incursion since 1838. The British Empire (three times) and Russia made the previous attempts. Their achievements included killing many Afghans, getting many of themselves killed on two occasions, losing, and winning only to find that they once they had left, they had no real influence on domestic affairs. They left hardly a trace in the sand.

### Ethnic groups

Afghanistan has been Muslim since 882. Its impassable mountains and desert terrain contribute to an ethnically diverse population. Pashtuns are about 42 percent of the population and occupy about 40 percent of its territory, mainly in the South. Tajiks, Hazaras, and Uzbeks, who collectively make up about 45 percent of the population, dominate the North. They have little in common but are capable of cooperating against the Pashtuns. The other 13 percent are divided among smaller groups but each has a locale it can fiercely defend. The population as a whole will not tolerate a permanent foreign military presence, however much a particular faction may welcome a temporary foreign ally (CIA, 2010; Vogelsang, 2002).

### The war of 1838 to 1842

Barfield (2010) gives a good account of Britain's three Afghan wars. After 1809, Britain began to fear that Russia would use Afghanistan to advance on British India. The competition for influence that was to cause the country such misery was called the "Great Game". In 1838, Britain decided to invade Afghanistan to place a puppet on the throne in Kabul. They succeeded briefly but in 1841, there was an insurrection. Ghilzai tribesmen massacred 2,000 British troops, 4,000 Indian troops, and 10,000 members of the families of troops in snow-bound mountain passes. One Englishman made it back to India, a Dr. William Brydon.

## The war of 1878 to 1880

In 1878, Kabul refused to accept a British mission (Russia had envoys there). Britain sent 40,000 troops and occupied much of the country. They defeated three attempts to drive them out, and left in 1880 with a friendship treaty, control over Afghan foreign policy, and control over the mountain passes to India. The Emir, Abdur Rahman Khan, subsequently defeated the Pashtuns and tried to disperse them throughout his realm. He maintained as much unity as is possible in Afghanistan: he had the allegiance of most tribal leaders and established control over the cities.

## The war of 1919

In 1919, King Amanullah sought to unite the country behind a war of independence. He attacked India but was soon defeated by British air power and was perturbed when they bombed his home. Britain was war weary and effectively conceded both independence and Afghan control over their own foreign policy. In 1928, the Afghan King and Queen received honorary degrees from Oxford. How could it be anything but downhill from there?

## The war of 1978 to 1989

On 27 April 1978, communists led a military coup in Kabul. Decrees about land reform and marriage customs brought civil war that spread throughout the country. In December, the USSR invaded. Over ten years, despite an army in the field that averaged almost 100,000, a huge advantage in modern weaponry, and air supremacy, they could not subdue the rebellion. Both Northern and Southern ethnic groups were largely opposed to them. They managed to kill somewhere between 600,000 and 2,000,000 Afghan civilians, and over five million Afghanis fled their country. Soviet dead came to about 15,000 (Maley and Saikal, 1989).

## *The war of 2001 to the present*

It is hard to tell whether the neo-cons who controlled US policy before Obama were ignorant of the dismal history of European intervention in Afghanistan or just thought that today things are different. Even now, they object that we cannot simply leave and "hand over the country" to the Taliban, as if any European power has been able to hand over this country to anyone.

The word "Taliban" obscures the facts. The insurgents that gained ground in 2008–2009 were united neither by tribe nor religion. Some are religious extremists, some tribal guerillas, some financed by drug lords. Their fragility was apparent when the "Taliban" leader in Musa Qala, deep in the Pashtun heartland, switched sides and became a local governor. They are a far cry from the homogeneous Taliban government that once ruled. That government allowed Osama bin Laden to establish bases. However, there is some question as to how firmly committed even they were to Osama bin Laden. After 9/11, clearly terrified of an American invasion, they said: (1) That they were prepared to try him, if America provided evidence of his involvement; (2) That if America was not satisfied with the trial, they were ready to find another Islamic way of trying him; (3) That they were willing to consider a trial in another country (CNN, 2001; CBS, 2001).

If the UN troops go home, the "Taliban" will control an enclave in the South. At present, al-Qaeda is happy with its new home in Pakistan. It is likely that most of the Afghan insurgents realize that the price of allowing such bases is American retaliation, and would prefer to fight only against the government in Kabul. If they are foolish enough to permit a base somewhere, it can be taken out by air power. There will be some "collateral damage" but nothing like the civilian casualties that an invasion causes.

## What America will leave behind

President Karzai has little power outside the capital and his government is riddled with corruption. The US chastises him, ignoring the fact that patronage is a matter of survival. He named 25 to serve in his Cabinet, but parliament approved only 14, claiming the others are either incompetent or corrupt (Hurst, 2010). Some MPs are sincere, but others just feel that their constituency has not got its fair share of the graft. A recent UN report says that the President's half-brother has been accused of amassing a huge fortune from the drug trade. The people are convinced that food aid has been either embezzled or diverted (UNAMA, 2010). The economy has become so dependent on foreign aid and the military presence that withdrawal will mean a severe recession.

So much for prosperity, what above stability? Hoffmann (2009) emphasizes that neither the government nor the insurgents can win an outright victory. He notes that 90 percent of the Taliban are not focused on international terrorism, but on defending their traditional turf against foreign invaders as all Afghans have for 3,000 years. Perhaps the two sides will share central government, and accept a regional autonomy that reflects Afghanistan's different tribes and ethnicities. The Pashtun/Taliban would rule in the southern regions of Helmand and Kandahar. The Tajiks, Hazaras, and Uzbeks would retreat into their traditional Northern territories. The central "government" in Kabul would include some Pashtun elements.

Even since 1700, the history of Afghanistan has been the story of the balance of power between the Pashtun and the Northern tribes. To interrupt that history for a decade or so at the cost of over 1500 American lives (and at least 20,000 Afghan lives), plus waging an expensive war when America could least afford to do so, was folly. It was an even greater folly than Iraq because Iraq at least had a history of strong, if repressive, central governments. It also has one cohesive group, the Shiites, that comprise 60 percent of the population and can provide a central government with majority support.

## Obama and Libya

Just to clear the air, popular support for intervention in Libya rests in part on the perception that Gaddafi masterminded the 1988 bombing of a Pan Am flight that killed 270 people. A Libyan intelligence officer was convicted of the crime and in 2004, Libya paid compensation. Few took seriously her denial of guilt or her assertion that compensation was the price for getting rid of the crippling sanctions imposed upon her (Miles, 2007).

Today lawyers, politicians, diplomats and relatives of the victims are convinced that the conviction was a miscarriage of justice. The UN observer (Köchler) wrote that "the guilty verdict was arbitrary, even irrational" and opined that it was pervaded with an air of "international power politics". The crucial witness was unconvincing (Pierce, 2009). He was paid $2 million US dollars (and his brother one million) under the "rewards for justice" program. The US denies that he was promised the money before hand. America wanted to punish Gaddafi for his anti-US and anti-Israel posture and her regard for the truth was negligible.

It is encouraging that Obama has shown little enthusiasm for the French and English crusade to unseat Gaddafi in Libya by using "NATO" air power. Perhaps he has developed some empathy with the Middle East. It is a pity that Europe has not been militarily weaker than Islamic states over the last three centuries. She might have profited from periodic military interventions to set things right: an Islamic army rampaging around France to correct their behavior toward the Huguenots, another in Britain to make them more benevolent toward the Irish, a third in Spain to make than offer independence to the Basques.

Obama had to do something in Libya to deflect attention from his compliant attitude toward US allies suppressing popular movements. His statement of 19 May 2011 (Landler & Meyers, 2011) on the Middle East reflects his embarrassment. America favors democracy in the Middle East, but not a word about the Saudis moving into Bahrain to crush popular protest against the local despot, only abandoning Mubarak in Egypt when it was clear that his position was hopeless, saying nothing about the fact that his fall has not displaced the military dictatorship that rules the country (except to make them more partial to the fundamentalists), and so forth. America's dilemma concerning the democratic movements that swept the Middle East is, of course, a result of her policy toward Israel. At present, a bought dictator who makes only perfunctory criticism of Israel is considered such a precious asset that the US is happy to see him rule forever. Therefore, she cannot afford to be consistently pro-democratic in the Middle East.

---

### Box 15: Bin Laden's birth certificate

It is not well known that America disabled Osama bin Laden long before they killed him. The National Security Administration got his cell phone number and gave it to telemarketers. After receiving a call that said, "this is the second and last notice that the warranty on your vehicle is about to expire", he was disoriented for several months. Osama bin Laden was actually born in Hawaii, not Saudi Arabia as a forged birth certificate indicates. Now that he is dead the lie perpetrated on the American public can be exposed, including the dark forces behind the conspiracy.

## Obama and the war on terror

Obama has not as yet used his office to educate Americans about the realities of the "war on terror". The killing of Osama bin Laden underlined the obvious: to assassinate someone, you do not send an army after him that gives him plenty of time to hide but use assassins who operate clandestinely. If you are trying to break an undercover group you spy on it and infiltrate it. If you locate a training base for terrorists, you attack it rather than a whole nation (see Box 15).

Above all, he should point out the absurdity of the non-sequitur that can be used to disarm any criticism whatsoever: "The fact that no new 9/11 has occurred shows what we have done is effective." When everyone knows that if a new outrage had occurred, that fact would have been used to bludgeon into silence anyone who opposed the wars in Iraq and Afghanistan: "Now we see the folly of those who wanted us to go easy on terrorists."

## Ready to reason

What a refreshing change if Obama introduces a decade in which US policy does not outrage the minimal moral principles of post-national people. However, even if this occurs, for me there is no turning back. Conversion experiences are not easily reversible. The four traumas (in order of magnitude) that made me a post-national person are indelible: American support of Pol Pot; the sanctions against Iraq; the slaughter in Iraq; and the slaughter in Vietnam. The next step was to clarify my thinking. What follows is a critique of the very concept of nationalism.

# PART III

# The Post-National Era

# Chapter 7

# *Love of a nation*

Nationalism is one of a family of ethical systems based on love, in its case love of a nation. Like other members of the family, and indeed like all ethical systems, we have a right to ask two questions. What is it about the nation that is loved, and where is the evidence that this trait or these traits are actually possessed by the nation in question. All of us would pose these questions when faced with that close cousin of nationalism called racism. If someone says he has a deep affection for the white race, and perhaps a loathing for black people, we immediately ask, what it is that makes white people worthy of love? Certainly not their sheer whiteness. This would trivialize a racist ideology, just as a book reviewer would be dismissed if he told us certain books were worthy of preferment because they had a white binding.

Other ethical systems based on love are often less scrutinized because they are currently more respectable. But even the lover of God must face the same questions. We have a right to ask what it is about God she loves (perhaps benevolence) and if she knows of an existing entity that deserves the name "God". When Nietzsche said he admired supermen, he told us what he admired about them (creative genius) and at least tried to list some proto-supermen. Someone may tell me he loves unicorns. But I will want to know what he loves about them (perhaps a horn with medicinal powers) and where they are.

I will address German nationalism because it caused more suffering in our time than any other (any nation would do). So we put our two questions: what it is about Germany he loves; and what evidence does he have that the actual Germany matches the ideal Germany.

## Identifying the members of a nation

You can name the individuals you truly love, that is, your spouse, your children, your friends, and point to the intimacy of contact you have enjoyed with them. No one has personal ties with every member of a nation. Therefore, there is a preliminary problem: can the nationalist even identify or describe the group he claims to love? He cannot identify the group by referring to all those who exist within a nation state's borders or hold citizenship. A foreign conqueror might invade your territory, annex it, and abolish citizenship. He will have to define the group in terms of those who participate in its culture, speak its language, appreciate its literature and cuisine, or have the personal traits that characterize its people, bravery, honesty, Gallic wit, what have you.

We know the language gambit is a lie. No predator nation would have spared its victims if they had all agreed to attend a language school. As for what is an admired cultural trait, do you mean to exclude those Germans who like Russian novels, Italian opera, Finnish interior design, French painting, and Shakespeare? What of the fact that the mass of the people you count on to fight your wars do not care about any of German high culture and prefer escapist literature, Rap to Bach, McDonalds to the traditional cuisine, American jeans to the traditional dress, Benny Hill reruns to any other form of humor? As for admired personal traits, not the slightest effort is made to verify their presence: the social sciences are not used to discern how many Germans are braver than Turks, how many are more honest than Canadians, how many more are altruistic than Finns, and so forth. Everyone knows that no such survey will ever be made because its results would be embarrassing: too many negative findings among your people and too many positive findings among others.

It is not for nothing that historically all attempts to define "superior" national identity were appeals to fictions like "blood", race, a mythic past from which descent is claimed. None of these present any problem for falsification. The Nazi ideal type never gave reality even a nod. Hence the gibe, blond like Hitler, slender like Goering, and tall like Goebbels.

## Culture and its champions

Nonetheless, cultures do exist and differ and claims that one is superior to others have been common. I will divide imperialism based on such claims into two kinds.

First, the claim that your culture would benefit a conquered people. Those some thousand years distant from a conquest may acknowledge a historical debt. Some Europeans today feel grateful that their country was part of the Roman Empire, as a factor that included their people within the area dominated by the classical legacy. However, this should not blind us to the fact that the imposition of a "more advanced" culture on a "primitive" one means a radical change that replaces one kind of human being with another. It is equivalent to exterminating the members of the subject culture and replacing them with members of the dominant culture, for example, as when America overwhelmed indigenous Native Americans.

Today's Native Americans are not peoples who have borrowed from the culture of contemporary America. Their own culture is extinct, which means they are simply Americans, albeit with a sentimental attachment to languages and customs that are now relics without a cultural soil. When the French talked about bringing their culture to North Africa, they were never willing to clarify just what this meant. It seemed to be a daydream of Algerian clones of docile French peasants, happy to be ruled from Paris, and a few more students with dark skins studying Descartes at the Sorbonne. To spread your culture in this way is merely to spread it territorially, as if you sent settlers into an unpopulated area. People do not really value this kind of cultural expansion as such, that is, as distinct from valuing it as an extension of the power of their nation: pride that so much of the world map is tinted with the color of the British Empire.

Second, there is the claim that you do not wish to extinguish the local culture but merely to give its people the benefits of certain institutions like democracy or market capitalism. In today's world, this virtually forbids conquest as a means: cultural penetration is far more effective. America has converted much of the world's youth to its youth culture without firing a shot. It may be objected that you want to promote high culture, but invading another country does not increase the appreciation of Liszt rather than Saint Saens. Aggressors are hated more than entrepreneurs and engender more local resistance. Japan began to join the West long before it lost a war. India is now westernizing far faster than it did under British rule. The nationalist may be very unhappy about such cultural penetration and its consequences. It breeds nations like China that may cast your own nation in the shade, and domestic capitalists who export factories and jobs overseas leaving your own nation with a crippled manufacturing sector.

As for exporting language or details of culture, it is pleasing when a well-read visitor turns out to appreciate your nation's literature. But Irish have never seemed interested in whether Swedes learn a bit of Erse or read great Irish writers. If Ireland had the ambition and the power to assert imperial control over Sweden, no doubt every drum would beat out the message that she had a civilizing mission in Scandinavia. Are we supposed to believe that anyone really cares, except for reasons of trade, whether Bantu or Nepalese speak English, or French, or German as a second language, and prefer Buster Keaton to Alistair Sim and Fernandel?

## Love and its objects

This may seem to be an evasion. Why should the nationalist put forward claims that make him subject to falsification? Why not simply say he loves or admires all those who would identify themselves as Germans? In reply, if he says this, he claims to love people he has never met, and admire people of whose traits he is ignorant.

Let us look at some other emotions. Someone suspicious of a friend who always flirts with her spouse is in touch with the real world, but what if she says she is suspicious of everyone in Chicago and Omaha? Someone who says that he is angry with his neighbor makes sense, but what if he says he is angry with the Eskimos and the Amazonians? To say you love your spouse, your children, your grand-children, these are people you know, with whom you have had intimate contact. But to love all Germans, people you have never met and never will meet, is like saying you enjoyed someone else's dinner, or like calling jokes you have never heard funny.

To admire a friend's qualities, you must get to know her well. Can you say you admire the qualities of all Germans and remain in complete ignorance of the detail of their daily lives? To say such things is to make love or admiration into reality ignorers. To lose touch with reality is the greatest of sins against reason. We exempt love only because we revere it so much. We forget that claims about deep feelings are to be taken at face value only if they have real rather than fictitious or empty objects.

Our evolutionary history probably endows us with a capacity to identity with a larger group, as if its members were our immediate family. For millennia, we competed for survival with other people who identified in that way with their group. Groups that were smaller or weaker in identity did not survive to reproduce. This may have left us with a human race all of whose members are programmed towards group identities that have only this rational basis: we need this kind of irrationality to defend ourselves against those who are equally irrational.

That does not give love or fellow-feeling claims a license to kill. If we encountered Martians who were programmed to love unicorns and to believe they were real, we might assess them in several ways, but none would include a judgment that they were rational. Rather their nature forces them to be profoundly irrational. As for how we are to survive if our group identities are diluted in the light of reason, I promise that we will confront that problem.

## Knights, Germans, and hunting dogs

To all of this, the nationalist may say: "Why should I scrutinize my patriotism in the light of reason? It is enough for me that the German nation and German society exist. I know what society socialized me, I know which nation I love, which army is the German army, and that my duty is to aim my gun at Frenchmen rather than at my own comrades."

In reply, no doubt that is an accurate description of your psychology, but it is the last word only for those whose morality is pre-rational. At one time, all but a few were immersed in primary ties, that is, their whole personality and behavior was shaped by their social role. A serf was a serf, a knight was a knight, and that was all you were. It dictated your conduct and your duties and that was that. The question of whether that behavior was really right was incomprehensible given who and what you were. There are still some people like that today: people who have been socialized to hate black skin, and will join a lynch mob whenever they find one, because that is simply what they are. There is the Martian who has been socialized (or programmed) to love unicorns and will kill anyone who denies their existence.

You say that you will not reason about your moral principles. Therefore, philosophy need not apologize for being unable to reason with you, any more than it need apologize for its impotence faced with someone who will not reason about unicorns. Fortunately, since the Renaissance, the few who reflect about morality have become many. We suspect that you are in bad faith if you deny you are among them, as shown by your use of the word "socialized". No medieval serf or knight used that word because it implies an awareness of having been given a moral code to obey — and one therefore, in principle, subject to modification by personal choice.

No modern state treats its citizens as if they were the unreflecting product of evolution, like hunting dogs that simply leap at quarry when the horn is sounded. Caricatures of the enemy are posted showing them with buckteeth (Japanese) or huge noses (Jews) to convey their inferiority. If the traditional enemy happens to become an ally, suddenly the caricature turns into a rather noble looking creature. During the German-Japanese alliance the two pictured one another as if they were morphing into a single physical type. Before you attack, a pretext is invented. The attack is a pre-emptive strike needed to ward off a threat, no matter how enfeebled the "enemy". Ideally, you are merely sending your soldiers as missionaries to overthrow a tyrant and do great good.

The point is not that these crude claims can be falsified, although, setting aside one case in a hundred, they can be. The point is that the "duties" or moral principles your socialization as a patriot has created can be tested against logic and reality. Once made explicit, they are inevitably appeals to cultural icons, or superior traits, or a love of a people that falsify reality. Every set of moral principles can be tested for whether its plausibility rests on sweeping some of what science tells us under the carpet. Those generated by nationalism are no exception.

### The sacred soil of my native land

There has been much talk in my lifetime about the "soil" of one's native land, the holy land of Ireland, the Biblical birthright of Israel, the sacred island of Okinawa, as if we were primitive agriculturalists tilling acres with which our ancestors and we have mixed sweat for generations. Before World War I, French troops would sneak at night across the border and, choked with emotion, bury their faces in the sacred soil of Alsace-Loraine, which had been annexed by Germany in the Franco-Prussian War. I always fantasized that the local farmers had brought in topsoil from the next province so that they really tasted the soil of the Rhineland.

If anyone starts listing the particulars of the landscape as something that give them reason for automatic obedience to their nation's dictates, perhaps the sublime emotions they feel when contemplating the Bavarian Alps, give them a photo interspersed with photos of the Southern Alps, the Andes, and the Rocky Mountains. Ask them to pick out the one that is so uniquely inspiring.

### Civic virtue

In showing that the nationalism that does so much harm is either pre-rational or irrational, perhaps we have proved too much. Human societies could not exist without bonds between their citizens that transcend enlightened self-interest. Pre-rational people are no problem because socialization will give them an unreflective patriotism. For a rational person, these unifying bonds must based on moral ties, such as a communal pursuit of justice, rather than personalized emotion.

I do not love my fellow New Zealanders or exaggerate their individual virtues. However, national societies, for now, are the largest human grouping whose people can cooperate to build humane societies. I ally myself with my fellow citizens to try to introduce single payer medicine, economic equity, antidotes to materialism, respect for the environment, and so forth. If few cooperate with me, I try again—foreigners cannot influence other polities, so New Zealand is the only moral arena I have.

The closer its people come to a shared pursuit of a humane society, the stronger my sense of civic virtue. The more "my" people prove themselves primarily interested in personal advantage, or in favor of policies that threaten others, the weaker. When I participated in American society, its arms policies seemed to me dangerous and posed the question of whether I should pay taxes, so much of which went for "national defense". New Zealand's tax revenue is spent mainly on necessary services and the welfare state and I have no sympathy with those who do not want to pay them. Civic virtue based upon a communal search for a just society or a less unjust world is a wonderful thing. Nationalism claims loyalty without regard to virtue. It has no more dignity than any other violent creed based on illusion.

Clarifying how a nation can attract my enthusiastic allegiance might convey a false impression, namely, that I am arguing against nationalism from a humane point of view. My reasons for endorsing a particular nation of course reflect my own moral principles. But my arguments against nationalism are non-partisan; indeed, some of them are encapsulated in Nietzsche. He too rejected the pretensions of nationalism ("patriotic drivel") and preferred another nation to his own (France to Germany). And his allegiance to a particular state reflected his principles, the extent to which it exhibited the ascendancy of supermen and their excellences. It was not based on whether he "loved" its members.

Needless to say, I may have many sentimental ties to individuals who have no higher aspiration than to earn more than their neighbors or use violence against other peoples. But I certainly do not respect them for this, much less love them for it. There may be excuses for what they do such as a media that distorts their perceptions of the world and what is worthwhile. They may, of course, win my regard by showing in the detail of their personal lives that they have virtues that compensate for their sins. There are also people I like simply because they are a delight to be around. And I, as much as anyone else, enjoy the sports, and amusements, and pubs that have become so familiar. There is nothing wrong with enjoying your national or local or ethnic culture. And being proud of its traditions, so long as they nourish the good or the morally permissible as you see it.

### Self-preservation

Self-preservation is morally permissible. We have posed the problem of how a person who has substituted civic virtue for blind patriotism is to survive. Today's rational person is adrift in a world organized into the equivalent of mobs of soccer hoodlums whose parochial passions blind them to the feelings of other peoples and make them capable of mindless violence. But a rational person's very existence is at risk if he or she is stateless. For sheer survival, you must belong to a mob for protection against other mobs. If your nation is attacked, and you want others to risk their lives for your defense, you must risk yours. If your nation happens by lucky chance to be in the right, as in the war against Hitler, you will fight with moral passion. If your nation is doing a great wrong, be a conscientious objector if that is allowed, discharge your gun into the air if you must serve.

In no way do I concede that the person who makes moral demands on his group will be any more hesitant to lay down his or her life than the pre-rational person. Thousands of union organizers, thousands in the civil rights movement, thousands of those all over the world who struggle against tyranny have been rational people fortified by the perception of a moral evil. When your principles draw a battle line between "us" and "them", you will find that you too are a product of your evolutionary history, and that plenty of ferocity is lurking behind the civilized façade. Moral actors do not lack courage. They just have to believe that what their nation is doing is at least morally permissible; and that is a very good thing.

This qualified commitment to one's nation will not, of course, satisfy some. It falls well short of the ideal held up to me as a schoolchild when we all read *The man without a country*. A young man named Philip Nolan, during his trial, angrily shouts "Damn the United States! I wish I may never hear of the United States again!" Upon conviction, the judge sentences him to exile, with no right to ever again set foot on US soil, and with no mention ever again to be made to him about his country.

The climax of the story is when Noland, after years of exile on US naval vessels, finally breaks down and addresses the following lunatic tirade to a young officer: "For your country, boy," and the words rattled in his throat, "and for that flag" and he pointed to the ship,

> never dream a dream but of serving her as she bids you, though the service carry you through a thousand hells. No matter what happens to you, no matter who flatters you or abuses you, never look at another flag, never let a night pass but you pray God to bless that flag. Remember, boy, that behind all these men . . . behind officers and government, and people even, there is the Country Herself, your Country, and that you belong to her as you belong to your own mother. Stand by her, boy, as you would stand by your mother!

Well. Apparently, we can understand someone becoming disillusioned with family or church or even with his or her God — but one's country — it is just unthinkable. I hate those who support arguments with psychoanalysis but for once, I will break my rule and cite Freud: the more stern the prohibition, the stronger the temptation to do the thing prohibited. What person of conscience in Nazi Germany could refrain from disillusion with his native land? What person of conscience in interventionist American could refrain from at least second guessing his nation's military involvement in lands whose "suffering" (which we feel so deeply) we ignore: at least until they are transformed overnight from allies into enemies.

## Harmless group identification

None of this means I cannot identify with a national sports team and cheer them on. I root for New Zealanders in the Olympics and for the national rugby team (the All Blacks). To care about one side turns an exhibition of skill into a competition. Some people have to place a bet to give the outcome an artificial significance. I do not bet, but to enjoy a prizefight on TV, I tend to identify with the older man (now that I am old) and hope he will be the victor. But I am fully aware that I am taking advantage of my programming toward group attachment to inflate the significance of the event. When nationalists go to war, what they do and the spirit in which it is done is incompatible with self-awareness of this sort. They must take their group attachment as having the full value their emotions place upon it without discounting their "love" of a people as a myth in the sense of having a fictionalized object.

## Nationalism and racism

No one denies that some people really do love their nation any more than one can deny that racists really do love their race (and hate all others). But both are reality-ignoring loves. Both racist and nationalist extend in-group fellow feeling to millions of people about whom they are ignorant. It may be said that races have no organized political existence. Very well, imagine that skin color groups were the sole political actors on the world scene and that there is no concept of a nation. There is no concept of China, rather simply of an organized Chinese race some of whom have "defected" to join other races. Would that make claims about race any more rational? It is just that nationalism still surrounds us and blinds us to what it really is, while history has stripped racism of the camouflage of respectability.

I have argued that the justification of nationalism entails reality denial. What nationalism actually does to people in terms of severing their ties with reality is indisputable. For evidence, see the chapter on "War fever" in Elon (2002). It details the extraordinary welcome accorded World War I by German intellectuals from Thomas Mann (who had long felt the need of a war to subordinate materialism to "German *Kultur*") to Rilke (the resurrection of "the God of hosts") to Max Weber ("this war is great and *wunderbar*"). Even the saintly Martin Buber, who later opposed the identification of Zionism with Jewish nationalism, lost his mind: "I know personally that Belgian women amused themselves by putting out the eyes of wounded German soldiers and forcing buttons ripped from their uniforms into the empty eye sockets." (Elon, 2002, p. 319).

## "Love" of mankind

Finally, I want to make it clear that I do not substitute one reality-ignoring love for another, that is, replace love of one's fellow citizens with love of mankind. Everything said about one of these "loves" applies to the other. Those whose humane ideals are based on ignoring the unlovable traits of humankind, those who must believe that every worker is a proletarian hero, or that peasants always sit under oak tress deciding wisely, or that women would be perfect if uncorrupted by men, have built on sand. My principles are based upon a lively outrage when one human being is victimized by another. The victim can be a dour Bible quoting assassin of what is joyous in life. Justice can encompass the anonymous in a way love cannot. Individuals do not have to be worthy of love, or even known to me, to champion their cause.

## What we owe

I do not owe my native land unconditional obedience or accepting illusions that exaggerate its merits. No mature moral agent can offer those to anyone. I owe my native land civic virtue and gratitude for providing me with a safe haven from barbarism and conquest. I owe myself moral integrity and rectitude.

# Chapter 8

# *An America one could love*

America once hoped to edify the world with the example of a nation exempt from the myopia and vices of the great powers of the classical European tradition. We have reviewed the behavior that has disillusioned Americans at home and friends abroad. How might the US revise its thinking and play a global role that would command respect?

To maximize the appeal of my sermon, its language will be that of moral realism (with the occasional quotation from Thomas Hobbes). I recall my dismay as a student when my lecturer Hans Morgenthau attacked idealism in general, and Wilsonian idealism in particular, as a possible basis for American foreign policy. Later I understood what he meant: that ideals had to be firmly grounded in political reality. What I will propose is not politically realistic in the sense that there is much chance of American policy makers accepting it in the near future. What I wish to do is sound an alarm that American foreign policy has lost contact with the real world, and that there is no remedy for its failures until that is remedied.

## World sovereign versus great power

We stand at a unique moment in history. American power dominates the world scene and she is surrounded by nations ready for leadership against a common enemy: the threat to well-being posed by weapons of mass destruction whether in the hands of nation states or actors who answer to no nation state. America has a choice: it can either play the role of a good world sovereign who rules by consensus; or merely behave like a victorious great power who treats the whole world as a sphere of influence.

The emergence of a single great power offers irreducible advantages. A great power looks no further than its national interest and imposing its own chosen moral goals. But better one of these than many. When there were two, the US and USSR, each could point to the other as enemy and justify force to seek advantage and pursue self-defined moral goals within its own sphere of influence. When there were several, the US, Russia, Britain, France, Germany, Italy, and Japan, each did mischief in its immediate vicinity and colonial sphere (Kennedy, 1987). As Hobbes said, better to have power invested in one actor because one appetite demands less than the insatiable appetites of many. Even America's power is limited and fewer need fear arbitrary behavior with so many eliminated from the game of great power.

However, a world sovereign can make the world better still. In particular, it must not do whatever it believes to be right if that is destructive of consensus. A world sovereign has a higher moral purpose: to make peace wherever possible and to consolidate and consensualize its rule. This means creating a certain state of mind. A great power can function if it is feared. To be a good world sovereign, you must win respect not because others fear you but because they fear what the world would be like without you. Here are a few propositions about the role of world sovereign in the hope that America will become a gracious king, perhaps not one who rules with our loves but at least one who rules with our grudging regard.

## A world sovereign must expect to be hated

Americans often ask why their country is hated. Ever since 1983, the US has yearned for the day when a global missile defense system would make it invulnerable to attack from any other nation. While this is not fully possible, America's enormous capacity to retaliate offers a pretty good substitute. It has also developed a military technology that allows it to kill whoever it wants, at least in the developing world, without serious loss even to its own professional military personnel. In the Gulf War, US casualties were 760 of which only 148 were combat deaths (Stat. Sum). A prolonged war is considered costly if it extracts a few thousand dead. This is something new and astonishing in modern history.

Imagine that Mexico had invented a force-field that rendered it utterly invulnerable and a death ray it could use anywhere on earth. It might use its power only for things that were unambiguously good, such as taking out American mayors who are incurably corrupt or those Los Angeles police who are undeniably racist (that is, it could do America the favor of enforcing US laws where America itself has failed). It might even give America a miss and take out the Saudi royal family and the North Korean elite. One thing is certain. A wave of fear and loathing would sweep America. Every resource and mind would be mobilized to discover how to break that force field and neutralize that death ray.

Add to this that America has used its power to take sides in morally ambiguous situations like the Middle East, that it has invaded nations in its sphere of influence when its construction of its interests so dictated, that it has instituted and supported governments whose citizens have suffered much, and it takes a moral blindness quite extraordinary to wonder why it is hated.

However, the point is this. A world sovereign that has these powers, and that has come to the throne by conquest (winning the Cold War) rather than by institution (consent), will be hated however circumspect its use of power. It can seek to minimize the world's animosity but it must not sulk if unloved. Assuming office requires some psychological preparation as every politician knows.

## A world sovereign should rule by consensus

How can America go from simply being feared towards a world in which most nations are far more afraid of what the world would be like without America's preponderant power? The primary goal must be "to make peace wherever possible", that is, to show that American power is indispensable to protecting nations and peoples from the most horrific forms of violence. Such a goal if pursued sincerely and realistically will maximize consensus for your rule. Its realization involves two tasks: eliminating the weapons of mass destruction that other states possess; reducing the threat posed by the privatization of such weapons.

It is sometimes asked how America can justify eliminating the nuclear weapons of others while retaining its own. The answer is that the emergence of one power with overwhelming military might provides an instrument that can eliminate nuclear weapons. Universal disarmament is not a practical option. Were all the weapons to disappear tomorrow, the knowledge of how to create them would survive. Within a few years even more nations would have them than at present: newcomers would be encouraged by the fact that they were not already hopelessly outgunned. Realistic steps toward control of such weapons are first, that America acquire an effective monopoly; and second, that its weapons be internationalized rather than destroyed. Postponing the second step, we will discuss the first.

What might reduce the number of those who currently have nuclear weapons? The first priority should be in South Asia where both India and Pakistan have weapons of mass destruction and a history of conflict. America should ascertain whether they are willing to at least let their systems atrophy, in return for an American guarantee of their security (see Box 16). It would have to be established that both are willing to (tacitly) accept that the present division of Kashmir is tolerable, when weighed against the possibility of nuclear devastation and the waste of ever-expanding nuclear establishments.

---

**Box 16: Hamid and 9/11**

A remarkable novel by Mohsin Hamid (2007), *The reluctant fundamentalist*, shows how constructive a role the US could play in defusing nuclear tensions between these two nations: "Surely, all America had to do was to inform India that an attack on Pakistan . . . would be responded to by the overwhelming force of America's military" (p. 143). It also portrays how tense the last confrontation between India and Pakistan was, what with spouses and children leaving the country. And finally, it shows how someone with deep roots in America's way of life was eventually overcome with rage at near absolute power and its abuse: "your constant interference in the affairs of others was insufferable" (p. 156); "the lives of those of us who lived in lands in which such killers [terrorists] also lived had no meaning except as collateral damage" (p. 178): "[when the twin towers collapsed] my thoughts were not with the victims . . . I was caught up with the symbolism of it all, the fact that someone had so visibly brought America to her knees" (p. 73).

---

America would have to guarantee that it would automatically come to the aid of whichever side was attacked; and probably head an international force that would take over border control if incursions by irregulars remained a problem. India could hardly disarm unless she was also guaranteed her border with China, and China should be asked to give firm assurances (as distinct from being asked to disarm).

We now see why the preservation of the US deterrent is essential. It must be there to give guarantees to those who might forsake their own. It must exist so that the US can seek the pacification that is the essence of the role of a world sovereign: "Covenants, without the sword, are but words" (Hobbes, 1958, pp. 154-155).

North Korea was willing to let its nuclear program wither thanks to its implicit non-aggression treaty with the US (Carnegie, 1994). It wants ratification of a formal non-aggression treaty by the US Senate, and the US should jump at this chance to demonstrate that it truly is pursuing a pacific policy. There is supposed to be a special relationship with Britain, which might, for the first time, be turned to some use. How salutary it would be if Britain were to unilaterally forgo nuclear weapons to prove to the world that US policy is not merely to disarm non-whites.

It may be that the time is not yet ripe for real steps toward nuclear disarmament. That is not a prescription for inaction. The intervention in Bosnia not only had humane consequences but also showed that America really did care about saving Muslim lives (Halberstein, 2001). It would also be good if America offered the world some kind of leadership in energy conservation and climate control. Submitting to the jurisdiction of the International Criminal Court would provide other nations an example of good citizenship. Until the US takes itself seriously as a world sovereign, it can hardly expect anyone else to do so.

Even the best policies may take time to build the necessary faith that America is sincere and committed in a way that would survive a change of administrations. That is no excuse for what we have got. Nothing could be worse than using the rhetoric of pacifying the world to justify behavior that shows that the rhetoric is a sham.

The pretence that Saddam Hussein posed a global threat or a threat to the United States undermined US credibility in a way that only time can repair. As for 9/11, every knowledgeable person knew that Iraq had no hand in this and if anyone should be invaded, it was America's ally, Saudi Arabia. That nation's citizens supplied most of the al-Qaeda cadre who attacked the Twin Towers. It had made no effort to restrict the recruitment of terrorists within its own territory, and it allowed "Islamic charities" to divert millions to international terrorists. How can anyone trust America's sincerity after it has debased high purpose into propaganda, simply to panic its citizens into a war pursued for other reasons.

Then there is the Korean debacle. Oddly, naming North Korea as one of the three most wicked nations in the world, and proceeding to attack another of the nations so named, made North Korea think it might be next (Bush, 2002). So they have flexed their nuclear muscles and what message has America sent to the world? If a state does not in fact have the weapons or delivery systems to threaten US interests, it is subject to invasion on moral grounds. While if a state actually has them, it will be treated with great circumspection. What an incentive system to offer nations (like Iran) who are unsure of America's intentions.

As for the struggle against organizations who have powerful weapons and are beyond the control of nation-states, and who therefore cannot be deterred by threatening a nation-state, they will have to be weakened mainly behind the scenes by cloak and dagger operations. These groups are such a threat to France and Germany, as well as America, that those nations will not withhold cooperation, despite the extraordinary language the American administration has directed at them over their unwillingness to invade Iraq.

Nonetheless, who would have thought America could have sowed so much disunity among nations who after the events of 9/11, were united in a common cause. The great harm that has been done is that none of these nations, nations who should have been among the easiest to bind together, is likely to feel for decades that they can trust American probity or continuity of purpose. None of them are likely to develop a consensus that real leadership can be expected from America as world sovereign, as distinct from merely tolerating her as the world power that emerged triumphant (thank heaven) from the struggle with the Soviet Union.

While international cooperation has the best chance of minimizing the threat to America from the above networks, nothing can guarantee security. Hopefully, the next attack on the US homeland will not bring a witless invasion somewhere to prove to the American public that "something is being done". The Byzantine Empire had to live for a thousand years without hysterical response to cities being periodically taken out by plague, the Bulgars, the Arabs, the Turks. An empire worth its salt will learn to respond rationally rather than by the politics of theater.

### A sovereign should not be so evil as to always do good

Individuals can kill to do good whenever they can square it with their consciences. Great powers operating within their sphere of influence can usually do whatever they have convinced themselves is good (it rarely is of course). A world sovereign does not have the right to do good indiscriminately.

Since the advent of the Nuclear Non-Proliferation Treaty in 1970, America has claimed the role of world sovereign. The very definition of sovereignty is control over the means of organized violence, and America claims the right to license those who are reliable enough to be allowed weapons of mass destruction. This imposes a set of rules. First: when the sovereign chooses an ethical goal, it should be one that commands an almost universal moral consensus. Second: if you break this rule, recognize that you have forfeited the right to do good.

America has sided with Israel in the Middle East. In 1948, the US was not a world sovereign but a victorious great power acting out of sympathy for a people who had done much to win a place in our hearts. As the reader knows, I do not propose that the commitment to Israel's survival should be abandoned. Still, the fact remains: America took sides in a morally ambiguous dispute. Having sided with Israel, America forfeited the right to do good in the Middle East. There can be exceptions, of course. If a nation attacks across an international boundary, and if there is a genuine consensus in the Arab world that the aggressor should be opposed, America can intervene, as in the case of the Gulf War.

But siding with Israel absolutely forbids intervention to promote "regime change" in the Middle East. It is absurd to expect Arabs to view America as a morally neutral sovereign who can be trusted to judge who should and should not rule. What they see is the hand of Israel, calculating who is or is not a threat to her security. America's first priority in the Middle East is to convince Arabs that she is as solicitous about their interests as she is those of Israel.

America says she wants democracy in the Middle East. However, she has more friends among the undemocratic elites of Arab nations than she has among the masses. The masses are unlikely to get democracy but they may get elites that better reflect their mood; and that mood is anti-Israel and anti-American. Does America really want more populism in Saudi Arabia or Pakistan? The notion that more popular governments would serve America's interests in the Middle East is too silly to merit discussion (see Box 17).

It is not even clear that a populist Iraq will be welcome. Ethnic sentiment may divide Iraq into three states composed of Kurds, Sunni Arabs, and Shia Arabs respectively. An independent Kurdish state would destabilize Turkey (Phillips, 2004). An independent Shia state would be an ally of "evil" Iran. America may find herself allied with the very Sunnis who sustained Saddam Hussein in power.

Better outcomes are possible. The politicians may find a viable compromise between Shiites, Sunnis, and Kurds, rather like Lebanon in happier days. The nation, or two-thirds of it, may be held together by an authoritarian government dominated by Shiites. Regimes may emerge better than that of Saddam.

**Box 17: Comic opera and the Middle East**

This is not to imply that America's attempts to buy friends among the elites of the Middle East have been productive. They have been as fantastic as the plot of a Gilbert and Sullivan comic opera. First, billions were given to Saddam Hussein in Iraq to arm him against Iran, then billions to Israel to arm her against Saddam Hussein, then millions to the Taliban to arm them against the Russians, then billions to invade Afghanistan to overthrow the Taliban, then $20 billion to Saudi Arabia and $30 billion to Israel to arm them against who — Iran or one another? It is true the Saudis will pay for their arms although Israel will not.

America keeps trying to pick winners in an area where no nation has guaranteed stability of regime except Israel and Turkey. Reflect for a moment as to how much better off everyone (including America) would be if we had never sent any arms whatsoever to the Middle East (or overthrown any regime in the Middle East). It is not too late to change. We could save a lot of money just by admitting that pumping arms into the Middle East has only one predictable consequence: everyone will feel they need more.

Well, are not such historical accidents to be welcomed — why look a gift horse in the mouth? Who cares about the depth of America's concern so long as the consequences are good? The answer is that a world sovereign must care about the world's perception of its aims. Invading people for their own good is calculated to reinforce the perception that America has not really abandoned the behavior of a great power. Other nations fear that granting America a license to interfere whenever there is a suffering people really means giving America a license to kill. Surely the task of the sovereign is to reassure, not to create alarm.

The sovereign must earn the right to use war to do good by compiling a record that inspires confidence. It inspires confidence by showing that it really does want a world made safer by the taming of weapons of mass destruction. That may take a very long time. Indeed, it may be only at that distant day when the first priority of the sovereign, a safer world, has been attained that the next priority, using force to promote the general welfare, can be persistently pursued. As usual, there will be exceptional cases. The sovereign may intervene when suffering is so great (Somalia) or slaughter so great (Bosnia) that much of the world forgets its suspicions. But when suspicion exists, the sovereign, however great its disinterested passion to do good, must show moral restraint.

America has shown no restraint. She has intervened in a region in which she is hated. Setting the Middle East aside, military intervention elsewhere has engendered fear rather than respect, look at her record in Latin America. The very fact that she uses the rhetoric of regime change shows how little she understands the priorities of a world sovereign. The excuse of every great power throughout history for invading weaker nations has been concern for the welfare of their peoples. Oddly, that concern is never manifest 10 years before the invasion or 10 years after.

At present the world is the most primitive kind of political system. Reforming government behavior should be near the bottom of the sovereign's priorities. A sheriff in a town where everyone carries a gun does not expend his political capital to reform the town drunk, despite the fact that it would be ideally desirable is help his wife and children. A world sovereign must subordinate every other good to its proper job: make peace wherever possible.

## A world sovereign should watch its tongue

Misplaced rhetoric in the cases of North Korea and Iraq has done harm. The rhetoric of the so-called "war on terror" has become almost universal. That rhetoric creates enemies that are not true enemies and friends that are not true friends. Worse still, it mis-educates the American people about the true state of the world.

Terror occurs when people both suffer from a burning sense of injustice and cannot compete with whomever they see as their oppressor in terms of conventional military tactics. Those are prerequisites rather than sufficient conditions: things like oil money and favorable terrain help turn discontent into action. The alternative to terror is massive civil disobedience after the manner of Gandhi and Martin Luther King. Sadly circumstances rarely allow for a pacifist response.

American irregulars were denounced as terrorists at the time of the American Revolution. Those loyal to the Crown who fled to Canada were not seeking a more temperate climate. American patriots could not get at English living in England. It would be interesting to know what would have happened if they had possessed the means. Two Prime Ministers of Israel, Menachem Begin and Yitzhak Shamir, were once members of terrorist organizations, namely, the Irgun and the Stern gang (Tessler, 1994; Quandt, 1993). The only way to stop terror everywhere would be to eliminate a sense of injustice or grievances everywhere. That is beyond the power of any world sovereign.

Therefore, the American people have been mis-educated about the true state of the world: they have been told that it can be divided into normal human beings and crazy people who out of sheer wickedness use terror. That premise entails the conclusion that everyone who is threatened by terrorists must be worthy of support, whether it is Israel fighting Palestinians, Russia fighting Chechens, the Philippines fighting Moslem rebels. American's knee-jerk response, that it would help the Philippine government "because they have a terrorist problem", shows how such absurd rhetoric can be hijacked by states the justice of whose cause America should carefully evaluate (Bush, 2003). The only terror America should oppose is terror that threatens America and those nations whose hands are relatively clean.

It may be said that there was no alternative to the rhetoric of the war on terror to energize the American public. That is nonsense. The Twin Towers was an attempt to destroy America's moral and political autonomy by inflicting cruel loss. It threatened the capacity of a free people to seek any goal abroad that anyone might resent. For domestic consumption, the fight against al-Qaeda should have been called "The Second War for American Independence". Other nations should have been asked whether they wanted America to be so crippled and whether they wanted to circumscribe their own autonomy out of fear. For international consumption, the objective of the joint effort against al-Qaeda could be called "freedom from fear".

No sovereign should give its subjects a fundamentally false picture of the world. A short-term gain in terms of emotive language is not worth the price. The farther the people are from a true apprehension of reality, the harder to sell policies that attack real evils.

## A world sovereign should be prudent when pursuing self-interest

No one expects America to be a saint, if only because a saint cannot play the role of world sovereign. Naturally, the US feels threatened with collapse because of lack of oil. Does she fear that developments in the Middle East are in the offing that might put all of that oil in hostile hands? It would be refreshing if something so clearly within the spectrum of normal great-power behavior were the true objective of the war against Iraq. However, an assessment of consequences shows that this may well not be the best way to ensure a flow of oil to the West.

The dangers are: (1) Such a Western military enclave might become even more hated than Israel; (2) Every regime in the area would be forced to take sides and if they remained US allies, the very regimes America fears may be overthrown will be overthrown; (3) Militants may make determined efforts to sabotage oil fields, refineries, and pipelines with incendiary devices.

Would it not be better to moderate American policy in the Middle East and depend on the desire of even regimes with limited sympathy for America to make money? That means selling oil on the international market for the best price you can get—with America having the advantage of being the biggest customer with the best hard currency.

However, let us assume that the pros and cons are evenly balanced on whether war or moderation is the best bet. If that is so, and if the world sovereign sees that war is undermining the consensus necessary to gain respect as world sovereign, that should tip the balance in favor of moderation. There is no sign that American governments believe that such consensus counts as even a feather in the scales. Lining up support is a grudging concession to the fact that a lot of people, quite inexplicably, seem to either withhold support or at least care about the extent of support. After all, support should come automatically because US policy is so admirable; if a majority of nations disagree, well so much worse for them. Sometimes, the recalcitrant are told that ways will be found to punish them for their cowardice and cupidity.

## A world sovereign should conciliate a "rival"

The greatest challenge that faces America is to be psychologically prepared to treat another nation as an equal. I refer to China, whose expanding economic power will eventually mean that any American endeavor to pacify the world will have to meet with Chinese approval. The first steps are to allow China to find her own way toward liberalization of her politics, and to do whatever is necessary to promote mutual understanding and trust. Above all, America must not play the great power game of treating China as a prospective rival that must be placed at a disadvantage.

At present, the US is flirting with a strategy of encircling China. This is to be done by a military alliance with India plus the crescent of bases extending from Pakistan through Southeast Asia up through the Philippines, Japan, and Korea. Why exactly, do we want to antagonize China needlessly? She has no serious overseas territorial ambitions. Her military forces are third rate. America's bases in the Far East have not been seen as too provocative thus far. China understands the historical reasons that have made Taiwan into an American protectorate and is willing to wait for the inevitable "Hong Kong" solution. The fact that Japan is an American protectorate in return for not being a nuclear power itself is actually reassuring to China. The US itself would like to reduce its commitment in Korea. The danger is that the alliance with India signals a whole new strategic role for these bases that will embitter China.

Can America never look at the world through the eyes of anyone else? Imagine a circle of Chinese bases that ran from Central America through the Caribbean through Long Island into Canada. But of course we are different because we have no aggressive intent. America's highest diplomatic priority should an unspoken agreement with China about what bases she should retain in the Far East. America should be nice to China in the hope that it can cooperate with her as joint world sovereign when the time comes. A pity America is not wining her trust by behaving like a world sovereign today.

### A world sovereign should seek to internationalize its power

America has long treated the UN as a mere instrument of national policy. When it could not get its way in the 1980s, it crippled the UN by withholding funds. In Iraq, the US did the UN a great favor: it took enforcement of that body's own resolutions out of its hands without its consent. In fact, as everyone knows, vigilante justice is the most direct path to undermining a government's authority and the one thing no government that wishes to survive can tolerate. Americans have been told that France and Germany are cool toward the US posture toward the UN. In fact, they think America is behaving like an outlaw that threatens the international system. Their mouths are shut by fear. The world cannot afford to insult the only nation that can play a dominant and constructive role in world affairs (Dyer, 2002).

The US should be obsessed with an overriding objective: how to render world sovereignty tolerable and productive. It must somehow sugar the bitter pill of a particular nation acting as world sovereign. Therefore, above all, it should be solicitous toward the UN.

Showing respect for the UN is a heaven-sent opportunity to offer proof that America looks forward to the day, however distant, perhaps a century away, of putting its power under international control. That depends, of course, on its having met the test of slowly pacifying the world through use of its nuclear and military superiority, persuading other nations to give up weapons of mass destruction and neutralizing those who would privatize them, thereby creating a world that it can trust and that reciprocates that trust. It can justify its pursuit of a nuclear monopoly only by sending a consistent message that those arms are a heavy burden it will someday be willing to share: that it will move to international control of its weapons of mass destruction once their pacifying purpose has been achieved.

Current arms policy aims at winning miserable small-scale advantages. I refer to America's refusal to ratify the Comprehensive Nuclear Test Ban Treaty, the sabotage of the Biological and Toxic Weapons Convention, and worst of all, the announcement that America considers itself free to use nuclear weapons against states that do not possess them

(Nye, 2002). The weapons named are tactical rather than weapons of mass destruction. But no tactical advantage is worth the anxieties that have been aroused.

## All of the lessons rolled up into one

The one lesson: practice moral restraint to achieve a higher moral purpose. There is precedent for America playing the sovereign role of offering security to nations who forgo weapons. America has said that an attack on non-nuclear Japan will be deemed to be an attack on itself; America has long guaranteed the security of weaponless Iceland.

If that policy is to be extended, with great caution, to other states, fears must be alleviated. The greatest fear is that as America comes closer and closer to total dominance and others come closer and closer to being at its mercy, it will abuse its power to impose its own self-interest or self-defined moral goals. The roles of world sovereign and Don Quixote are incompatible. Every lesser moral goal must be assessed in the light of the overriding goal of a safer world. Is that not good enough to satisfy the most voracious moral appetite? (See Box 18).

---

**Box 18: Vision for a new Iraq**

Bush tried to do good according to his own lights. Shortly after the invasion of Iraq, he issued the "Vision for a New Iraq" whose draft constitution contained an anti-abortion clause. Evidence of a happy correspondence between radical Islam and the President's moral principles.

---

The problem with American foreign policy is not so much that the US is acting out its own version of the role of a great power, national interest modified by idealism, with the familiar mix of intelligence and stupidity, genuine moral purpose and blind moral arrogance. It is that America is playing the role of a great power at all. Rather than the role history has assigned it, namely, that of world sovereign.

Things could be worse. What if the USSR had won the cold war? What if history had nominated France, a nation whose intelligent cynicism forbids any long-term objective of a better world order? Then there is Britain, a nation so addled by its "special relationship" with America that it has lost any capacity for independent thought. To be fair, Britain is experiencing that prolonged nervous breakdown that afflicted Sweden in the 18th and early 19th centuries when it had to face the fact that it was no longer a great power. It is a pity that Britain has developed no higher goal that to be the jackal that runs at the lion's feet.

America must choose. It can exploit its position as the sole great power, treating the entire world as a sphere of influence, baffled by the world's failure to applaud its good intent (when it exists). Or it can play the role of world sovereign. To settle for the former is to settle for being a dwarf in giant's clothing. To choose the latter means being a good and prudent king, unloved, envied, resented, but acknowledged by all to be essential to security and well-being.

## A postscript on history

Why does America find the psychology of a world sovereign so alien? Partially because every great power finds it alien. But American history adds some specificity to so general an explanation.

The US policy elite is no more exotic than the Mandarins of China. American history has dictated the contents of their minds and like most Americans, they are too a-historical to assess their heritage. Two huge nations, isolated and virtually self-sufficient, 19th century America and imperial China. Both self-obsessed each looked into the mirror and saw a unique human experiment with a people and institutions specially blessed. The Chinese court could not imagine why anyone would want to visit the barbarians and sixty percent of US Congressmen see no reason to possess a passport.

After World War I, the view that America was the center of the universe spit into two ideologies. American liberals tended to espouse Wilsonian idealism, that is, they believed that America had a mission to democratize the world beyond its borders. If this failed, the presumption was that other great powers were too wicked to lay their interests on the altar of a better world (Krock, 1992). But there was at least the breath of a psychological constraint: a sense that there was something odd about imposing a democratic world order by undemocratic means, that is, through force rather than a consensus that embraced at least a fair swag of other nations.

American conservatives tended to be isolationists. They found the rest of the world so wicked as to be hopeless. That was a very powerful psychological constraint: America should not risk contamination by associating with bad company but should concentrate on perfecting its own society (Cole, 1962).

Today's architects of intervention combine the worst features of both ideologies. The conviction that the world is wicked is held with all of the fervor of the conservatives. This erases the liberal constraint (never very strong) that other nations should be persuaded. The crusade to improve the world is espoused with all of the fervor of the liberals. This erases the conservative constraint that America should focus on perfection within. The result is something rather incredible. America claims the right to cure all of the world's ills by force. And the stated rationale for this claim: the rest of the world should simply acknowledge America's unique virtue.

I would be the last to object to the fact that America's psychology has a moral dimension. But there is kind of self-esteem that easily translates into moral arrogance, particularly when a nation becomes aware that it possesses great power. Self-esteem is a virtue only when it has a solid foundation. A combination of idealism and realism brings self-esteem under control. It implies a balance sheet that weighs up when we have put our ideals into practice with self-restraint and rationality against when we have ignored them or made cheap moral gestures. That is usually a humbling experience. Otherwise, you are likely to get the worst possible combination: moral arrogance endlessly expanding to fill a cognitive vacuum.

# Chapter 9

# Americans who would be good

This chapter will address what role individual American citizens should play if they have become post-national people and believe America should live up to its rhetoric about acting as a world sovereign. However, first I wish to make clear that the post-national psychology, the shift of allegiance from the United States to humanity, has no monopoly on personal integrity. The odor of sanctity is always repugnant. Contemporary America has many other psychologies worthy of regard. I will acknowledge five and the list is by no means complete.

### The veterans of foreign wars

Americans who have fought in wars like Vietnam and Iraq fall into two groups: those who became disillusioned with the civilians that sent them there; those who did their duty as soldiers with pride. Many in both groups have returned maimed in either body or mind. It is up to them to talk to each other, and we should proselytize only if they come to us. It is not the place of those who remained safe at home to lecture brave men and women about ethics. Moreover, no democracy wants an army that is not obedient to elected civilians.

Every person has a bottom line below which they feel they have forfeited their integrity and if, while on duty, a general or a private comes to believe that their war cannot be defended, they will resign as a matter of principle. It is pity that the general can do so with impunity while the private faces court martial. But everyone who acts within the rules of war deserves honor. Those peace demonstrators who hurled insults at members of the armed forces should reflect about their motives. Every mob loves a moral license to intimidate individuals.

## The traditional patriot

Harry Truman was an honorable man and there are millions of Americans like him. I have a not too distant relative who is not political but honest, sane, and responsible. His family and all of his friends know they can depend on him. Before any intellectual patronizes him, let them earn the same accolade. His major recreation is hunting (I do not think he is a member of the National Rifleman's Association). We enjoy watching sport together. When the subject of opposition to the Iraq War arose on TV, he remarked that if we had not fought Hitler, we would be speaking German today. He trusts his government to define who his nation's enemies are and would answer any call to arms. He is like Cephalus in Plato's *Republic*, a decent man who tells the truth, pays his debts, and does his civic duty. No nation can survive without his virtues. I have no interest in trying to change his psychology for mine. On the other hand, America's policy elite are fair game.

## Americans who have known tyranny

I have friends and colleagues who fled Eastern Europe as it was under Stalin and revere America in a way that few of its native-born citizens can imagine. While attempting to be human in societies riddled with informers and strangled by the totalitarian mind, they saw America as the powerful champion that offered some hope of eventual deliverance. Those who came to America felt they had been transported from hell to heaven.

Czeslaw Milosz (1953) wrote a great book, *The captive mind*, about the psychology of intellectuals behind the iron curtain. In his chapter, *Looking to the West*, he records the scruples of Polish intellectuals who were affronted by America's "vulgarity". He challenges their elitism: "Yet a girl working in a factory, who buys cheap mass-production models of a dress worn by a movie star, rides in a old but nevertheless private automobile, looks at cowboy films, and has a refrigerator at home, lives on a certain level of civilization that she has in *common* with others." America was the first society to offer the mass of people this kind of liberation. Call it "vulgar", but it was something beyond the dreams of a woman working a collective farm near Leningrad.

His chapter, *The lesson of the Baltics*, gives a preview of what would have happened to all of Eastern Europe if Stalin had proved eternal. Resistance to collective farming was broken by thousands of cattle-cars loaded with people headed toward uninhabited areas of Russia. Whole villages stood empty, Russian settlers were ordered to replace the missing, Russian became heard on city streets more often than the native languages. A letter from a deported family, ostensibly about their daily life, said in disguised script: "Eternal Slave".

I do not want to be a moral snob akin to the intellectual snobs Milosz portrays. To speak to those from the East about America and Pol Pot, or American sanctions against Iraq, seems obscene. They know what governmental brutality is really like and are angered at what they see as moral hypochondria. In response, I cannot challenge the integrity of their experience and the psychology it has created, necessary once for hope, now an expression of gratitude. But all psychologies do not have the same potential to benefit a humanity faced with a dangerous and anarchic world. America thinks quite well enough of itself without adulation, and self criticism is a prerequisite if her potential for good is to be realized. To ask of America only that she be much, much, much better than Stalin, is to ask too little. I am unwilling to surrender that much of the realm of the moral.

## The conservative tradition

A negative assessment of America's use of force beyond its borders is not peculiarly radical or even liberal. Right and left is a division having to do mainly with domestic politics. American conservatives often criticize the wars America has fought over the last 120 years As a touchstone, I will use a recent book by Thomas Sowell (2009), a thinker far removed from my views on domestic politics, but someone I respect because of his respect for evidence. A shared reverence for the truth often overwhelms all else.

Sowell expresses what is best in the conservative tradition: suspicion of any elite that pretends to know better than the people affected what laws, institutions, and social arrangements are appropriate for them. He details how intellectuals try to improve the lot of the poor without knowing any economics, and have regulated prices, rents, and wages with counter-productive results. He notes how the market is far superior to a "command economy" in that it leaves decision-making to those who actually participate in economic life, consumers, workers, employers, the actual residents and owners of rental housing, all of whom may be presumed to know more about their options than a central planner.

He opposes judicial activism as a matter of unelected judges rewriting the US constitution in the light of their ideals, blind to the fact that law is a structure resting on accumulated social experience as to how to regulate conduct. He notes gratuitous interference with the family, with how each family allocates roles in terms of gender, discipline of children, and so forth.

The principles he elaborates have application to American foreign policy, particularly military expeditions abroad. Although Sowell does not mention them, I am reminded of how unjustly historians have treated the so-called "isolationists" that existed in America before World War II. They are often painted as know-nothing non-interventionists. In fact, they often had a sophisticated line of analysis, which emerges when we look at that eminent conservative, William Graham Sumner.

## The Spanish-American War (1898)

Sowell (2009, p. 205) quotes President McKinley's defense of annexing the Spanish colonies of Cuba, Puerto Rico, and the Philippines: "They are children and we are men in these deep matters of government and justice." He castigates all those who favored America's precipitation of this war, laying bare their assumption that they knew how to improve the lot of other peoples, and points out that this war engendered a whole series of overseas interventions that had nothing to do with America's national interest.

William Graham Sumner (1899), the leading conservative thinker of his day, made a detailed case as to why the war with Spain was wrong. On January 16, 1899, he delivered a speech to the Phi Beta Kappa Society of Yale University. He called the Spanish-American War "The conquest of the United States by Spain" by which he meant that while America has won the test of arms, Spain had won the battle of ideas. He advised the citizens of the Republic to think carefully about jettisoning America's traditional ideals in favor of the imperialist mentality of Spain. He anticipated two of Sowell's themes.

**Manipulation of public opinion by intellectuals.** "It was necessary to make appeals to the public . . . (and) such appeals were found in sensational assertions which we had no means to verify, in phrases of alleged patriotism, in statements which we now know to have been entirely untrue." The American public was give the impression that the sinking of the US battleship *Maine* in Havana Harbor was due to a Spanish mine, when in fact it was either an accident or done by the Cuban rebels acting as agent provocateurs. It was also necessary to salve the consciences of those who were uncomfortable with explicit endorsement of imperialist ideology: "Senator Foraker has told us that we are not to keep the Philippines longer than is necessary to teach the people self-government." That of course justified a period of domination limited by nothing other than the mindset of America's elite.

**Lack of local knowledge.** "We assume that what we like and practice, and what we think better, must come as a welcome blessing to Filipinos. This is grossly and obviously untrue. They hate our ways. They are hostile to our ideas. Our religion, language, institutions and manners offend them. . . . The most important thing we shall inherit from the Spaniards will be the task of suppressing rebellions." Also: "It is impossible to improvise a colonial system. . . . It depends on a large body of trained men, acting under traditions which have become well established, and with a firm esprit de corps."

**Consensus.** Sumner and Sowell are correct. The Spanish-America War was one based on hubris and illusion. The aftermath was terrible. America refused to turn the Philippines over to the indigenous forces led by Aguinaldo who, by all reports, had restored order and schooling in the areas he controlled and had widespread popular support. The ensuing war lasted 14 years and killed an estimated 200,000 to 1,500,000 people. The US imposed a government that took upon itself to disestablish the Catholic Church as the state religion, and make English the primary language of government and some businesses. What American of conscience could support such a brutal and unnecessary war? Mark Twain founded the Anti-Imperialist League to organize opposition.

## World War I (1917-1918)

Sowell points out how little justification can be offered for America's entry into World War I. The primary case was that a German submarine had sunk the *Lusitania*, a passenger ship that had Americans on board. However, the war had become a contest between Britain and Germany as to who could use naval power to deny the other side war materials and food. The British used surface ships to blockade ports, while the Germans used submarines. The former could give warnings before attack and let passengers and crew disembark, while the latter could not: if they gave away their position, the threatened ship could wire for warships to come and sink the submarines.

Despite this, America insisted on the right of its citizens to sail into the blockaded ports. Sowell notes that it was revealed, years later, that the *Lusitania*, a British passenger ship, was actually carrying hidden military supplies. This was common practice and for the Germans to ignore it would have made a mockery of their blockade.

I will simply add that the Kaiser was not Hitler. World War I was a dynastic war between European nations in which the US had no legitimate reason for choosing one side over the other and no interests at stake. Aside from the English sympathies of some of its people, the only discernable motive for US entry is that President Wilson and others saw it as an exciting and pivotal historical event, whose outcome was likely to redraw the map of Europe and much of the colonial world, and just could not bear to stand on the sidelines.

## World War II (1941-1945)

Who could dispute that the overthrow of the Hitler regime, and the need to beat Hitler to the acquisition of nuclear weapons, were objectives that commanded the support of anyone of conscience? Those who did not perceive that it was necessary to use military force to neutralize Hitler before the war, or defeat him during the phoney war when he was preoccupied in the East, and those who thought that he might establish some sort of civilized regime they could admire, were mistaken with consequences that were beyond tragedy. Sowell is quite right that reluctance to confront

Hitler and admiration for him did not neatly divide right and left but cut across the political divide.

## The cold war (1945-1991)

I have had my say on this. A policy of rational deterrence was justified with emphasis on the word rational. A policy of mindless accumulation of weapons was not, and dogmatic opposition to any government abroad that stood to the left of the Democratic Party was not. There is much debate about whether Reagan won the cold war by his proposal to develop a Missile Defense System (Star Wars). Whether or not this proposal was effective is a question dependant on insights into the thinking of the Russian elite no one has. But I will say that if it worked as claimed, it was because the Russians were stupid.

Gorbachev's mentor Aleksandr Yakovlev (1992) says that it played no role at all. Yet, when Gorbachev spoke at a session of the Politburo in October 1986, to justify his decision to offer Reagan a 50 percent reduction in nuclear arsenals, he said that if Russia attempted to compete in the new round of the arms race, "the pressures on our economy will be unbelievable". On the other hand, after this speech, Gorbachev asked Yevgeny Velikhov, his chief science adviser, to evaluate whether Reagan's Strategic Defense Initiative would pose a threat. Velikhov replied that the project was fanciful, and that the Soviets could deploy additional offensive missiles to saturate the Star Wars system much more cheaply than the United States could construct additional defenses (Kaplan, 2004).

Who knows whether Gorbachev believed him, but Velikhov was correct. If the USSR had been smart enough, and determined enough, and Reagan had been foolish enough to persist, it would have been the US that was threatened with bankruptcy not the USSR. The strategy:

(1) Express despair about Star Wars and get the US to build the thing. There is no evidence that it would

have worked and the cost would have been enormous.

(2) Shift some of your own expenditure to nuclear submarines. Even if Star Wars had worked, it did not have the potential to take out low-flying missiles fired from submarines within a few hundred miles of America's coast.

(3) If after 30 years of enormous expense, the system became effective down to the water's edge, smuggle about 50 agents into America with small but potent nuclear "back pack" devices capable of taking out US cities. The US cannot even prevent millions of tons of drugs from being smuggled across its borders

In sum, the USSR did not have to match US spending on Star Wars to have an effective deterrent. It only had to remain sane while the US undertook absurd and ruinous expenditure. Whether those Russians who saw this convinced others, I do not know. But Reagan's military spending program should have provoked hilarity in the Kremlin. Russia could have prolonged the Cold War by at least another generation.

## The Korean War (1950-1953)

Sowell does not discuss this case. It is one that deeply troubles me. I was 16 when it began, and did not arrive at a mature judgment at the time, as I did a decade later when America began to invest its prestige in Vietnam. I did look at the evidence about how the war started and decided: that it was a clear case of North Korea attacking South Korea; and that there was no indication that any substantial proportion of South Korea's population welcomed unification on North Korea's terms. They simply marched a conventional army into the South and tried to conquer it. That was enough for me.

As I aged, I became aware of the evidence that Stalin had beefed up the arms of the North Korean Army just prior to the attack. Later evidence showed that Kim Il-sung might have convinced Stalin that he could conquer South Korea in three weeks. This renders unconvincing the main piece of evidence used to argue that Stalin was unaware of Kim's intention; namely, that the USSR was absent from the UN Security Council (she had boycotted it) when it voted to come to South Korea's aid. The argument is that if Stalin had known about the attack, the USSR would not have missed a chance to cast a veto. But if the war would take only three weeks, Kim's victory would have been a fait accompli whatever the UN did. While I did not think an emboldened Stalin would march into Austria and Italy, it was salutary to deter him from any expansionist ambitions he might have.

I was also suspicious of the kind of dictatorship being established in the North by a man who had changed his name to mean, "become the sun". I was of course not aware of what a nightmare his regime would become after the mid-1960s when he introduced "Juche" as a substitute for feeding his starving people. The essence of Juche is that Kim Il-sung and his son Kim Jong Il (whose own son has just succeeded him) have bathed Korea with light and warmth so satisfying that the sun is a mere candle by comparison. Kim Jong Il wrote a poem that captures its flavor:

> The sun rises on the sea buoyant,
> The land glows under the sun radiant.
> Stars twinkle with nocturnal grace
> In my father the General's embrace.

My disquiet is, what if Vietnam had come before Korea and not after? Would I have convinced myself, on the evidence available at the time, that the difference between the North and South Korean regimes was not enough to be worth a bloody war? I hope not, but I will never know. With the advantage of hindsight, I would have been tragically mistaken.

## The Vietnam War (1961-1972)

Sowell (2009, p. 247) expresses no opinion on whether US participation was justified, but focuses on other themes, the influence of intellectuals on events, whether the war was winnable, and its bloody aftermath. I have already detailed our differences in Chapter 4, and therefore will merely repeat that it was the aftermath of the war (support for Pol Pot) that was above all indefensible.

## Iraq and the Middle East (2003 – today)

This brings us to the current Iraq war. The neo-cons who steered US troops into Iraq had no roots in the conservative tradition. In late 2002, Sowell wrote a short article that says much on this subject.

He notes that even before 9/11, the neo-cons were pushing an activist "national greatness" foreign policy and seized upon that event to promote their agenda. He quotes Max Boot who wants America to use its "might to promote American ideals" around the world. As Sowell says, that used to be the language of Wilsonian liberals: "The very idea that young Americans are once again to be sent out to be shot at and killed, in order to carry out the bright ideas of editorial office heroes is sickening. . . . to destroy regimes that are trying to destroy us is very different from going on nation-building adventures" (Sowell, 2003).

This article was published some 10 weeks before the invasion, and Sowell's later book merely refers to "debatable issues about the wisdom of the invasion or the nature of its goals" (Sowell, 2009, p. 262). Therefore, I will elaborate on why those who take seriously the wellsprings of the conservative tradition should have opposed the invasion.

## Conservatives and social engineering

True conservatives suspect any elite that pretends to know better than people on the ground what is good for them, what laws they should have, what relationships are workable between ethnic groups and the genders. If there is anything that should be anathema to a true conservative, it should be the whole concept of nation building. They should call to mind the old conservative maxim: A fool can put on his coat better than a wise man can put it on for him.

At one time, conservatives were not susceptible to self-deception about those who would engineer "regime-change" out of concern for the welfare of other peoples (a rhetoric as old as Rome). That any significant group of Americans cares much about the lot of the peoples of Syria, or Iraq, or Afghanistan, or Iran, is about as plausible as that Americans are agonized with concern about the inhabitants of the highlands of New Guinea. Our hearts are touched when natural disasters occur. We give money, often generously, and get on with our lives.

But rather than allowing the Middle East to have its own history, the Bush elite knew how to do radical social engineering throughout the whole area. They knew that all of these nations had in place the social pre-requisites for a free-enterprise democracy, knew that overthrowing just one dictator would engender an irresistible trend toward imitation throughout the area, knew that populist regimes would be more friendly to the US and Israel, knew better than the Shiites whether they should have separation of church and state (shades of the Philippines), knew better how to manage the non-Shiite ethnic minorities, knew better than the Iraqis what steps would be tolerable enough to actually promote gender equality (rather that become dead letters), knew enough to draft an Iraqi Constitution (talk about judicial activism: remember the plank forbidding abortion), knew how to unite Afghanistan, how to free it of corruption, how to suppress the cultivation of opium, how to suck eggs. They have not yet decided to make English the official language of these two nations.

I have argued that America has priorities that come far ahead of regime change, particularly since her resources are not unlimited. But my point here is to appeal to the traditional conservative point of view: even if our hearts were pure, we do not know enough to go around the world and use war to regime change and nation build (engineer new nations). For every time we happen to do some good, there will be a time when we create a national disaster.

## Toward consensus

There is a group of historians meeting in what was once called Yugoslavia that consists of Serbs, Croatians, Slovenes, and so forth, with this agenda: each people has its own mythical version of history in which it is innocent and all others guilty of atrocities; they as responsible academics mean to agree on what the evidence actually shows without special pleading.

Perhaps I can offer a bald summary of America's record that democratic socialists, liberals, and conservatives can all endorse. As a preamble, I hope we can all agree that American history has not been dishonored by consistent wickedness. The decision to drop the Atomic bomb was made by honorable and prudent men who did what was thoroughly understandable at the time. The cold war was not America's fault. America contributed to crises with China (off shore islands) and Russia (Cuba) but these were matters of a president out of his depth (Eisenhower) and a new president (Kennedy) who soon did better.

As for recent wars, I offer the following as a basis for moral consensus:

(1) The Spanish-American War (1898), unnecessary with inhumane consequences;

(2) World War I (1917-18), unnecessary but perhaps shortened by America's entry;

(3) World War II (1941-1945), a matter of moral obligation;

(4) The Korean War (1950-53), at a minimum morally permissible;

(5) The Vietnam war (1961-1972), unnecessary with inhumane consequences;

(6)  Afghanistan, at least understandable initially but no excuse for a prolonged and futile attempt to nation-build;

(7)  Iraq, unnecessary with inhumane consequences, although perhaps no worse than Iraqi history would have eventually entailed.

In four cases, untruths were used to mobilize sentiment for entry into an overseas war: that Spain sunk the battleship Maine; that the Lusitania was an innocent passenger vessel; that small North Vietnamese naval vessels attacked the US Seventh fleet in the Gulf of Tonkin; that Saddam had concealed weapons of mass destruction. But this is mainly a reason for skepticism about what any government tells you when they want a war, and about whatever "intelligence" they choose to make public. A critical mind could have accepted all four false claims and yet opposed war as an inappropriate reaction.

The important point is whether we can agree on three things: that during the last 112 years, there has been only one brief period (the 20 years between 1941 to 1960) in which America's overseas wars were justified; that over the last 50 years, none of her major wars have been even morally permissible; and that over the last 20 years, her polices have been inconsistent with her proper role of world sovereign. If that is too much to ask, let me propose a minimal consensus. We all agree that: America has fought unnecessary wars (without being unanimous about those that qualify); these wars led to unnecessary loss of life; therefore, we are determined to define for ourselves who America's real enemies are; and we oppose nation-building crusades in favor of some more rational strategy of pacifying the world. My detailed scenario concerning the last is offered for criticism and debate.

### The modern patriot

I revert to my case for post-nationalism. The obvious reaction is to assert that Americans could share either the broader or narrower consensus without switching allegiance from the United States to humanity; and consequently becoming a post-national person is gratuitous. A stronger critique would be that those who abandon patriotism are morally remiss.

## *The world citizen as parasite*

Sowell (2009, pp. 275-280) points out the value of patriotism and a sense of national honor. Without these things, it is harder to mobilize support for the national preparedness necessary to safeguard America's security. With his usual acuteness, he isolates the shift of allegiance that my views imply: that citizenship of the world, and concern for the wellbeing of mankind, come ahead of national citizenship. He points out that there is as yet, no world government that can safeguard people's rights; and there is no place called the world, which exists outside the state system. Where is the place to which one can move and become a citizen of the world? He adds that to live in a nation and accept the benefits that citizenship confers, without accepting mutual responsibility to sacrifice oneself for national defense, is to be a parasite. In reply:

(1) The question is not whether to strip America of her capacity for self-defense or to refuse to participate in a war of self-defense. But when there is a consistent record of calling bloody wars fought overseas "wars of self defense" when they are not, except within an alternate reality created by an intellectual elite, at some point the citizen must baulk and say enough.

(2) I simply no longer believe in national honor without asking whether America is behaving honorably, or in a patriotism that overrides the question of whether American policy has anti-humane consequences. Assume that national honor and patriotism are beneficial its terms of America's unity and esprit de corps. However desirable these things may be in the national context, once your allegiance has shifted, you cannot command your mind and heart by such

considerations. National honor in the sense of winning a war is far less important than whether America is earning the kind of reputation for prudence and sobriety that would allow her to play the role of world sovereign. Unless her sense of self-worth helps to pacify the realm, rather than simply reinforcing polices that take humanity toward a world less and less secure, it is worthless.

It may be, all else being equal, that nations whose citizens believe in God and an afterlife (look at the suicide bombers) have an advantage over other states. But once you have lost your faith in God, you simply cannot manufacture personal belief because of its military value. I do not believe that anyone who has attained moral maturity can believe that patriotism meets the criteria that apply in moral debate (any more than racism can); and I do not believe that anyone committed to humane ideals can do less than demand that his or her nation stop taking the world further from a state of pacification. Just as you would have to prove the existence of God to convert me, you will have to prove my analysis wrong. I cannot believe what I cannot believe however strong the consequential arguments. I am a post-nationalist man and that is that.

(3) A halfway house would be that I (and like-minded intellectuals) keep my thoughts to myself. In the *Emile*, Rousseau is so disturbed by the possibility that loss of faith in an after-life will bring a plague of injustice, that he admonishes atheists to keep quiet. Aside from the fact that I think keeping quiet would do more harm than good, the notion of the members of a cognitive elite having a dialogue among themselves, one never shared with their spouses, children, or peers has so many bizarre ramifications that it must be rejected.

(4) Sowell acknowledges the plausibility of the historical hypothesis that intellectuals have one beneficial contribution to their credit, namely, the creation of nations out of lesser units (he thinks that they are doing the reverse today). Let us talk a bit about the unification of Italy.

Cavour was the political genius. He had deep roots in Piedmont and his native city of Turin. He introduced sugar beets and chemical fertilizers in its neighborhood. He never aimed at uniting the disparate states of Italy but at "unification" by having Piedmont absorb as much of Italy as possible. He went to the Turin Military Academy at the age of 10, but despite his patriotism, his liberal and modernizing tendencies made him suspect. Garibaldi was the military genius. He was born in the city of Nizza (or Nice), and was enraged when the House of Savoy gave the city to France to get French aid. Lincoln offered him a post as Major General in the Union Army, but Garibaldi demanded that he be made commander-in-chief and that Lincoln promise to abolish slavery (which at that time Lincoln was unwilling to do). How close America came to never having a President Grant (historical determinists note)! Mazzini was the intellectual genius behind *Young Italy*. He had his roots in Genoa. He got his law degree at 21 and collaborated with a local newspaper until the authorities closed it down.

At least Garibaldi and Mazzini, and all of their followers, were subject to the objection that there was no such thing as Italy, and that they had no place to go where they could be "Italian citizens", and that they were parasites who fed off the states of their birth while professing allegiance to a higher entity. Today, it is easy for us to dismiss such an indictment as fantasy. But transfer of allegiance from a locale to the nation state came to much of Europe only after the Napoleonic wars.

No charge of parasitism or allegiance to fictitious entities would have moved Garibaldi or Mazzini. They has shifted their citizenship in their own minds and it was impossible to transfer it back it to one of the states that made up the Italian peninsula. One of their main motives was pacification of the realm. As long as Italy was made up of petty states, French and Spanish armies would be free to march around and kill people to further their own interests. Needless to say, the world is not ready to be unified into one global state. But

America has told me that its role is to serve as a world sovereign and help the world's peoples survive the nuclear age. She has ignited a new allegiance in me and I am powerless to pretend otherwise, at least in my own heart.

## The world citizen as unnecessary

There may be Americans who are committed to humane ideals, who share the full rather than the minimal consensus I have stated, who even accept all I have said in this book about Pol Pot, sanctions against Iraq, and how America should perform the role of world sovereign. Yet they have experienced no shift of loyalties from America toward "world citizenship". Therefore, they have no inclination to call themselves anything other than an American patriot. If they think and behave like me in all ways, what is the cash value of calling myself a post-national person? This prompts me to reflect on how I differed before and after 1990.

The main differences: (1) I went from believing what my government said was *prima facie* true, toward a skepticism akin to my suspicion about foreign governments like Britain or France; (2) I went from trying to find extenuating circumstances for apparently immoral US polices to no more presumption of innocence than I would accord other non-totalitarian nations; (3) If America blundered in to a pointless war where only "national honor" was at stake, I would not continue such a war an extra day to salvage victory over defeat (wars are not games where one roots for the home team: they kill people); (4) I decided that nation-love justifies no preferment for any nation's behavior on the international scene, which is to say I could praise America only if her behavior contributed to a more peaceful world; (5) I became committed to a world sovereign of genuinely international character to which I would like to see America's sovereignty subordinated as soon as possible; (6) Looking back at when I had risked my life (or at least injury), I took more pride in causes with an international flavor like the sit-ins (racism is an international evil if ever there was one) than any risk America might have demanded of me over the last 50 years.

In sum, I became totally impartial in my assessments of America, the prospects for America's long term survival as an independent state, and "international" in the causes I thought most worthwhile. Naturally, I had more opportunity to do good in America because I lived in America. Naturally, I retained sentimental ties with America, for example, felt a special satisfaction when she acted well (elected her first black president). So I will now turn the question back on the enlightened American patriot: if you are like me in all of these things, exactly what is the cash value of calling yourself a patriot? Has not your distinctive allegiance to America been drained of content until, like the Cheshire Cat in *Alice in Wonderland*, all that is left is a smile?

Perhaps the difference between us is just how much sentimentality we retain about America. If so, that difference has little cash value, and we should not be a slave to words. You call yourself an American patriot with an internationalist perspective, and I will call myself a post-national person with ties to America. We will both be good citizens obedient to her laws except when she asks us to fight wars of empire. The US government knows how many of us there are and it, at least, lumps us together. It is frightened to draft men to fight its wars of empire. It gave up the draft in favor of a fully professional army in 1972, and what event does that year mark? The end of the Vietnam War. The US dares not risk the public rebellion it would incur if it issued draft notices.

## Intellectuals and their untruths

Thinkers who speak for traditional conservatism do the left a service by helping us recognize the sins of the liberal members of the policy elite. Read Sowell (2009) about how anti-Bush and anti-war intellectuals clouded truth in the debate over Iraq. But we on the left can do a similar service:

call attention to the sins of conservative members of the policy elite. (It goes without saying that Sowell and I are among the few intellectuals who always influence public opinion for the better.)

If ever there was a climate of opinion, dangerous because it made rational pursuit of America's interests impossible, created by politicians and their intellectual entourage, it was the pro-intervention discourse that preceded US entry into Iraq. When I speak of these distortions, I will call them untruths, rather than lies. People (some at least) feel uncomfortable saying the opposite of what they know to be true. What happens is that intellectuals use concepts to create an artificial reality that differs from actual reality, and since no one says anything except what makes sense within that artificial reality, it is mutually reinforcing and everyone speaks with enormous conviction and sincerity.

## The great untruths about Iraq

There were two outrageous untruths that colored the whole debate about the invasion of Iraq, namely: that Saddam Hussein was implicated in the 9/11 attack on the twin towers; and that he had significant links with al-Qaeda and Osama bin Laden. These were not only false but the opposite of the truth. As a secular regime, Iraq was preeminently the regime in the Middle East hostile to religious fundamentalism. Throughout the Arab world, Saddam and bin Laden were known to despise each other. Any al-Qaeda agent that Saddam caught would be hung from the nearest lamppost.

The invasion was launched on 20 March 2003. Polling data show that right after 11 September 2001, when Americans were asked about who was behind the attacks, only three percent mentioned Iraq or Saddam. By January 2003, a Knight Rider poll showed that 44 percent of Americans believed that either most or some of the September 11 hijackers were Iraqi citizens. The truth of course is that none of them were, and that 15 of the 19 involved were from America's "ally" Saudi Arabia. That poll did not establish that 44 percent of Americans thought Saddam had masterminded the attack. But it shows a shift toward linking Iraq with 9/11 that is quite remarkable. In February 2003, the link was shown to be explicit. A *New York Times*/CBS poll revealed that 45 percent of Americans believed Saddam was "personally involved" in 9/11.

If they had wanted an honest debate, the Bush administration would have stated categorically that the invasion of Iraq had nothing to do with 9/11. They would have rested their case entirely on whether a Saddam with weapons of mass destruction was a threat, and whether so wicked a regime should be overthrown. Bush's speeches actively encouraged the public to link Saddam with 9/11. This culminated in his press conference on the eve of the invasion, which focused almost solely on Iraq. Bush mentioned 9/11 eight times, and referred to Saddam Hussein many times often in the same breath with 9/11 (Feldman, 2003). He and his speechwriter were not naïve. They were attempting to reinforce the public's perception that Saddam had played a role in the attacks without telling a flat lie.

When you create an artificial reality, it comes to so dominate your mind that your speech betrays you. After the war was well underway, on Sunday 14 September 2003 at NBC's "Meet The Press" program, Vice-President Dick Cheney asserted that Iraq was the "geographic base" of the terrorists behind the attacks on New York and Washington. This was a tactical error in that it was so patently false that the press had to ask questions. Bush's response on the following Thursday is a paradigm of a state of denial.

He said that there was no evidence that Saddam had a hand in the attacks, and denied any attempt to confuse people about a link between Saddam and 9/11. To defend Cheney, he was driven to state another untruth: "al-Zarqawi, an al-Qaeda operative, was in Baghdad. He's the guy that ordered the killing of a US diplomat. . . . There's no question that Saddam Hussein had al-Qaeda ties" (Shepard,

2003). The facts: Abu Musab al-Zarqawi went to Iraq to have his leg amputated; there were unconfirmed reports that he then visited a remote region in northern Iraq, where an Islamic group affiliated with al-Qaida was encamped; this group, far from being an ally of Saddam, wished to replace his secular government with an Islamic regime. Perhaps the US should have helped Saddam encircle the group and liquidate them.

## The great silence about Israel

An alternative "reality" that cannot be laid at the door of the Bush administration is the climate of discourse about Israel, and the consequences of the US alliance with Israel. It is the creation of an American intellectual elite of all persuasions, left, right and center. Having said much about Israel, I will be brief.

The list of truths unsaid is long and bizarre: Israel does not simply want peace with her neighbors but demands that they accept piecemeal annexation of the West Bank; therefore Israel is resented not only by fundamentalists but also by moderate Arab opinion; although the US finances Israel, and thus its imperialism, at best it cannot moderate Israeli behavior and at worst does not care to; therefore, America cannot play a neutral benevolent role in the Middles East; Israel is not a valuable ally but a client state that entails mainly liabilities and few real assets; Israel's national interest is diametrically opposed to the modernization of the Middle East; when a populist Arab leader says that Israel should be eliminated, this only shows he is a politician; when an Arab leader attempts to break Israel's monopoly of nuclear weapons in the Middle East, it is not America's security but Israel's security that is under threat; the President of Iran is not a mad dog that wants nuclear weapons to attack Europe and commit national suicide; and he is not a magician who could embark on such a venture without other Iranians doing anything to restrain him.

## The potency of the foreign policy elite

I think I have demonstrated that the US president has enormous power over foreign policy, particularly when it comes to vetoing overseas adventures that are unnecessary and indefensible. It remains to evidence the power of America's foreign policy elite, that is, the intellectuals who are preoccupied with foreign policy, have a vision as to what it should be, and articulate their opinions at least to a circle of acquaintances. The best example is the war in Vietnam, although we should keep in mind that the duration of this war made it unpopular and therefore unusually subject to debate.

By 1968, the intellectual elite had turned against the war. They called the Tet offensive in January of that year a defeat. A few years before they might have called it a military victory that had decimated the Communist forces. Arthur Schlesinger, Drew Pearson, Walter Cronkite, the editors of the *Wall Street Journal*, Walter Lippmann, Joseph Kraft, and John Kenneth Galbraith said that the war was unwinnable or an endless stalemate (Sowell, 2009). The press in general downgraded the bravery of US soldiers and emphasized the few US atrocities (My Lai), while ignoring numerous atrocities by the Communist forces. All of this bolstered the esprit de corps of the North Vietnamese who knew that they lacked the "capability to defeat you on the battlefield" but expected to "win this war on the streets of New York". And made it politically impossible to continue the US troop commitment to Vietnam.

The language of the elite was colored by the fact that that they had made up their minds about the war. But I believe they were correct on the most important point: it was unwinnable unless America made a commitment out of all proportion to what was at stake. And it was good that intellectuals brought this war to a halt. I wish they had given a more objective account of Tet and had been more sensitive to the sacrifices of the US troops. But whatever their sins, they do not compare with those of the intellectuals of the previous generation. In my youth, Senator Joseph McCarthy and Richard Nixon and their intellectual admirers created a climate of opinion so absurd that you had to risk violence to hear Paul Robeson sing. I know: I was an usher with orders not to allow anyone to enter the hall who was armed.

Intellectuals are not the only culprits. Ordinary people mouth untruths about politics like crazy. The intolerance of "average Americans" toward having their "climate of opinion" challenged can be extraordinary. My own experience of this extends beyond addressing audiences in the American South about race in the early 1960s. I once addressed an international affairs club in a town largely populated by retired farmers. The advertisement for the talk included the names of the group's executive. Two worthy citizens wrote letters to the editor: "I wish it to be known that the John Smith who lives at 38 Apple Pie Road is not the same person as the John Smith who is a member of the International Affairs Club". After all, an honorable man must protect his good name.

Lying has escalated over the last 60 years, from a time when at least something had to be at stake, to a time when almost everyone lies just to avoid a minor social inconvenience, or even to save the trouble of saying a few extra words. I do not know what to do about this except to tell as few untruths as I can.

Setting lies aside, there is one kind of misinformation America can do something about: the misinformation that arises from American intelligence. Time after time, we have seen how error or a perhaps unconscious diagnosis of what the President wants to hear has led to mistakes: the prospects of overthrowing Castro; what happened at the Gulf of Tonkin; the existence of weapons of mass destruction in Iraq; the links between Sadam and al-Qaida or Osama bin Laden; the "threat" North Korea or Iran poses for Western Europe.

An utterly trustworthy power that is outside the inward looking culture of Washington DC should be selected to establish an intelligence review organization. Iceland seems an obvious candidate. It would select its own personnel subject to security clearance. Its members would be given all intelligence on which The CIA, etc., bases its Presidential advice and would be financed generously, so they can get independent intelligence to verify factual claims and form their own opinion about their significance. It would have the power to comment publically whenever it believes that anything in the public domain, from Presidential speeches to policy "leaks", is based on assumptions it considers invalid.

## Altering the thinking of the elite

How can we alter elite opinion and get post-national presidents (I do not expect them to describe themselves as such)? Given the mix that determines who will be the President, I can suggest no formula to manufacture ones who understand the implications of America's role as world sovereign. This does not mean we must trust entirely to luck. The foreign policy elite do not just create the intellectual climate that constraints a president: the president is often a member of that elite and programmed by its thinking. Eisenhower, Ford, and the younger Bush were not members, but Truman, Kennedy, Nixon, Carter, Reagan, the elder Bush, Clinton, and Obama qualify, and this is true of most presidents prior to Truman.

### A strange suggestion that would mean much

What I will suggest may seem trivial but I think it matters very much. I suspect there are at least a million adult Americans that have crossed the divide from nationalism to post-nationalism. The first step is to end their sense of isolation.

Everyone whose first allegiance is to the world community should wear a blue ribbon. You would see that other post-nationalist people existed and they would recognize you. When I was a child, a Catholic guest at dinner on Friday had to refuse meat to manifest their faith (it was not just vegetarians who were a pain in the neck). Think of the impact if thousands of dinner parties included someone advertising his or her "faith". You are likely to be asked why you wear a ribbon and, when your explain, you may find someone who is already a convert.

When your nation does something serious that cannot qualify as humane, or takes us toward a more violent world, you would replace your blue ribbon with a black one. There would be no test of who had the "right" to wear a ribbon. Each person would decide. There would be pacifists and non-pacifists, fans of the UN and its critics, fans and critics of Israel, fans and critics of Obama. No coherent voting bloc would emerge. The aim is something more fundamental: to change the climate of opinion about foreign policy, to be visibly there and ready to debate your position (see Box 19).

---

### Box 19: Blue arm bands

At one time, I suggested a more visible sign of allegiance like arm bands. This suggestion made me uncomfortable, and I have been on the line in the American South for racial equality when that was no joke. It made friends uncomfortable who dared pour blood on draft cards during the Vietnam War. I think each of us should ask ourselves why this is so. Do we reject it because it is really trivial, or because everyone has inhibitions about calling attention to themselves on a daily basis, and hates to be thought a political bore. Perhaps these "trivial" social sanctions are really more difficult to endure than the risk of a policeman's club?

---

I would wear a blue ribbon in New Zealand and a black one in America. It would be strange to wear black in America and not in Britain. Setting aside her absurd and counterproductive nuclear capacity, she usually reinforces America's determination to wage war overseas. Australia does the same. Swedes would have to decide for themselves whether her arms sales abroad are enough to go from blue to black. Swiss would have to decide what they think about the role of Swiss banks. Brazilians would have to think about what is being done to the Amazon. I think a lot of Israelis would wear black. The residents of other states ought to (a long list starting with North Korea), but the sanctions suffered would be prohibitive.

## A conventional suggestion that would mean something

If you are a scholar, write books. If you are a journalist, write articles and discuss your paper's editorial policy. If you are a teacher, there are discussions in the common room. If you are none of these things, there are letters to the editor and the chats you have with friends and associates.

It is a relatively small elite whose thinking needs to be changed. And remember, the nationalists know we exist. It is not just a matter of being afraid to draft young men for military service. Each time the US government tries to sell a counterproductive war as a war of self-defense, or as necessary to control weapons of mass destruction, their rhetoric becomes more frantic. They set the terms of a debate that we can win, so long as we speak out and are heard. They are actually issuing invitations to participate in a post-national debate.

I have ignored the deep causes that make America's presidents and elite what they are. The candidates range from the shadow of our evolutionary past, the territorial imperative, children of the enlightenment, the frontier, regionalism, the media as merchandiser, failure to appreciate that all identities are self-constructed, illegal immigrants dissolving the bonds that unite us, too many guns, banning prayer from the schools, using phonetics to teach reading, too much sugar in the tomato paste, fluorine in the water supply, the proximity of high voltage transmitters, and the influence of the hydrophobic orangutans of capitalism (see Box 20).

---

### Box 20: Poor Chiang-Kai-shek

How one misses the language of the old Radio Peking. My favorite was "the fascist bandit Chiang-Kai-shek". Chiang got it from all sides. In 1944, when General Joseph Stillwell was sent to oversee US aid to Chiang, he told a journalist: "The trouble in China is simple. We are allied to an ignorant, illiterate, superstitious peasant son of a bitch." (Ferguson, 2006).

---

Such things are probably too entrenched to manipulate. Reason, if that is what is present in this book, always counts for something.

Post-national people cannot just be political, they will also have to give moral advice to individuals. Given the record of the last 50 years, I would feel obliged to counsel any young person not to join America's professional army: killing in an unjust war is murder and they are likely to be a party to killing that cannot be defended. Does this mean that I would disarm America by stripping her of a professional army? Of course not. Long before any sizeable number of recruits were alienated, I would have altered the climate of opinion among America's policy elite in such a way that such wars were no longer fought.

### The road ahead

Will the disaffection of some intellectuals with nationalism spread to enough people, at least in the industrialized nations of the first world, to be effective? Who knows.

Nationalism was largely absent in Europe until toward the end of the Napoleonic wars, say about 1814. People were loyal to the dynasties that ruled them. When Napoleon invaded his "nation", Goethe said: "We all felt for Fredrick [the Great], but what did we care for Prussia?" (Goethe, 1811–1833). It was only in 1914, that the last bastion of dynastic loyalty, the Austro-Hungarian Empire of Francis Joseph, succumbed to the forces of nationalism (see the wonderful novel by Joseph Roth, *The Radetzky March*, 1932). Now, almost 2014, more and more thinking people in the West are replacing the state as moral authority with the concept of the ethical state, to which we owe total obedience only insofar as it treats the people of the world as its constituency. By 2114, nationalism may be no more influential than it was in 1814. It may be axiomatic that a thinking person is a post-national person.

On the other hand, a fierce competition for scarce resources (oil, water, habitable environments) may await us. Super-national loyalty is a luxury of the secure. In a savage state of nature, where all fight all to survive, the nation state is the only shelter from disaster.

As for me, America buried my heart somewhere near the Cambodian-Thai border. Other nations with a veneer of civilization have done things more wicked, what of Rome and the Greek city states? America has not degenerated into what Saint Thomas calls a "society of beasts" blind to the moral law. But this is the 21st century and, until I reached moral maturity, America was *my* country. She taught me a lesson to which there are no exceptions: nationalism is morally bankrupt and no one should be intimidated when it calls itself patriotism. We must learn to walk into history without following a flag.

# References

Acheson, Dean (1949). White paper on China. In *Department of State, United States relations with China, 1944-1949*. Washington DC: Government Printing Office.

Adams, Sherman (1961*). First-hand report: The story of the Eisenhower administration*. New York: Harper.

Agent Orange (2008). *Agent Orange homepage*. Retrieved June 11, 2008.

Albright, M. (2003). *Madam secretary: A memoir*. New York: Miramax.

Alsop, Stewart (1958). How we drifted close to war. *Saturday Evening Post*, December 13, 1958.

Arnold, J. R. (1990). *Tet Offensive 1968: turning point in Vietnam*. New York: Osprey

Arnove, A., ed. (2000). *Iraq under siege: The deadly impact of sanctions and war*. Cambridge MA: South End Press.

Baldwin, H. W. (1965). A critic of our Vietnam policy answers some questions. *New York Times* (International edition, weekly review), February 21, 1965.

Barfield, T. (2010). *Afghanistan: A cultural and political history*. Princeton NJ: Princeton University Press.

Barnet, R. J. (1960). *Who wants disarmament?* Boston: Beacon.

Bergen, Peter (2006). *The Osama bin Laden I know: An oral history of al Qaeda's leader*. New York: Free press.

Bibby, T. M. (1985). Vietnam: the end, 1975. *Small Wars Journal*, April 1, 1985.

Black, I., & Milne, S. (2011). Barack Obama lifts then crushes Palestinian peace hopes. *Guardian*, 24 January, 2011.

Bronner, E. (2008). Olmert says Israel should pull out of West Bank. *New York Times*, September 29, 2008.

Burnham, G., Lafta, R., Doocy, S., & and Roberts, L. (2006). Mortality after the 2003 invasion of Iraq: a cross-sectional cluster survey. *The Lancet*, October 11, 2006.

Bush, George W. (2002). State of the Union Address, January 29, 2002. See: www.whitehouse.gov/news/releases/2002/01/20020129-11.html

Bush, George W. (2003). Remarks to the Philippine Congress, October 18, 2003. See: www.state.gov/p/eap/ris/rm/2003/25455/htm

Carey, N. (1962). The history of disarmament. *New University Thought*, Spring, 1962.

Carnegie (1994). "Agreed framework between the United States of America and the Democratic People's Republic of Korea" of October 21, 1994. See: www.carnegieendowment.org/state/rpp/agreed_framework.cfm

CBS (2001). Taliban won't turn over bin Laden. CBS News World, September 21, 2001.

Chamberlain, L. H., & Snyder, R. C., eds. (1948). *American foreign policy*. New York: Rhinehart.

Childs, Marquis (1959). *Eisenhower: Captive hero*. London: Hammond.

CIA (2010). *The world factbook: Ethnic groups*. Washington DC: Central Intelligence Agency Publications.

Clifford, Clark, & Holbrooke, Richard (1991). *Counsel to the President: A memoir*. New York: Random House.

CNN (2001). World shock over U. S. attacks. *Cable News Network World*, September 11, 2001.

Cockburn, P. (2008). Sunni vs Shia: the real bloody battle for Baghdad. *Independent*, February 5, 2008.

Cole, W, S. (1962). *Senator Gerald P. Nye and American foreign relations*. Minneapolis: University of Minnesota Press.

Compton, Arthur Holly (1956). *Atomic quest: A personal narrative*. New York: Oxford University Press.

Conetta, C. (2003). *The wages of war: Iraqi combatant and noncombatant fatalities in the 2003 conflict. Appendix 2: Iraqi combatant and noncombatant fatalities in the 1991 Gulf War*. Project on Defense Alternatives Research Monograph # 8, 20 October 2003.

Cook, Fred (1961). The C.I.A. *The Nation*, June 24, 1961.

Cronkite, Walter (1968). Who, what, when, where, why: Report from Vietnam by Walter Cronkite. CBS Evening News, February 27, 1968.

Dean, V. M. (1948). Implications of the Marshall proposal. In L. H. Chamberlain and R. C. Snyder (eds.), *American foreign policy*. New York: Rhinehart.

Donovan, R. J. (1956). *Eisenhower: The inside story*. New York: Harper.

Dougan, C., & Fulghum D. (1985). *The fall of the South*. Newton, MA: Boston Publishing Company.

Druckman, M. (1962). America's new disarmament policy. *New University Thought*, Spring, 1962.

Duiker, W.J. (1981). *The communist road to power in Vietnam*. Boulder, CO: Westview.

Dyer, Gwynne (2002). UN goes along with charade. *Aljazeerah*, November 14, 2002. See: www.aljazeerah.info/Opinion%20editorials/2002

Elon, Amos (2002). *The pity of it all: A portrait of the German-Jewish epoch 1743-1933*. New York: Picador.

Esber, R. (2009). Under the cover of war. The Zionist expulsion of the Palestinians. Alexandria VA: Arabicus Books.

Failoa, Anthony (2006). In Vietnam, old foes take aim at war's toxic legacy. *Washington Post*, November 13, 2006.

Feldman, Linda (2003). The impact of Bush linking 9/11 and Iraq: American attitudes about a connection have changed, firming up the case for war. *The Christian Science Monitor*, March 14, 2003.

Feldman, Noah (2008). Vanishing act. *New York Times Magazine*, January 13, 2008.

Feldman, S., & Shapir, Y. S. (2004). *The Middle East strategic balance 2003-2004*. Brighton UK: Sussex Academic Press.

Ferguson, Niall (2006). *The war of the world*. New York: Penguin.

Fitzpatrick, M. ed. (2008). *Nuclear programmes in the Middle East: In the shadow of Iran*. London: International Institute for Strategic Studies.

Flynn, J. R. (2008). *Where have all the liberals gone? Race, class, and ideals in America*. New York: Cambridge University Press.

Flynn, J. R. (2010). *The torchlight list: Around the world in 200 books*. Wellington, New Zealand: AWA Press.

Franck Report (1946). A report to the Secretary of War. *Bulletin of the Atomic Scientists*, May 1946.

Freedom of Communications (1960). *Part I: The speeches of Senator John F. Kennedy, presidential campaign of 1960*. Senate Committee on Commerce, 87th Congress, 1st Session.

Friedman, A. (1993). *Spider's web: The secret history of how the White House illegally armed Iraq*. New York: Bantam Books.

Fulbright, J. W. (1963). *Fulbright of Arkansas*. Washington: R. Luce.

Gabriel, R. H. (1948). American experience with military government. In L. H. Chamberlain and R. C. Snyder (eds.), *American foreign policy*. New York: Rhinehart.

Garfield, R. (1999). *The impact of economic sanctions on health and well-being*. London: Relief and Rehabilitation Network (RRN) Overseas Development Institute.

Goethe, Johann Wolfgang von (1811 -1833). *From my life: Poetry and truth* (English edition: *The Autobiography of Johann von Goethe*. Trans. John Oxenford. Chicago: University of Chicago Press, 1974).

Goodman, W. (1990). Review/Television; Jennings says U.S. helps Khmer Rouge. *New York Times*, April 26, 1990.

Goold-Adams, R. (1962). *The time of power: A re-appraisal of John Foster Dulles*. London: Weidenfeld and Nicholson.

Gordon, Joy (2002). Cool war. *Harper's Magazine*, November 2002.

Graebner, Norman, ed. (1961). *An uncertain tradition: American Secretaries of State*. New York: McGraw-Hill.

Halberstein, D. (2001). *War in a time of peace*. New York: Simon & Schuster.

Halle, L. J. (1961). Lessons of the Cuban blunder. *The New Republic*, June 5, 1961.

Hanson, V. D. (2001). *Courage and culture: Landmark battles in the rise of Western power*. New York: Doubleday.

Hassan, G. (2004). Unmasked: The war against Iraqi children. *Information Clearing House*, August 3, 2004.

Hiltermann, J. R. (2003). Halabja: America didn't seem to mind poison gas. *International Herald Tribune*, January 17, 2003.

Hobbes, Thomas (1958). *Leviathan*, ed. Herbert W. Schneider. New York: The Liberal Arts Press.

Hoffmann, H. (2009). *Afghanistan: Negotiations with the Taliban as the path to peace*. The independent World Security Network Foundation, discussion paper, 07-Dec-09.

Hughes, Emmet John (1963). *The ordeal of power: A political memoir of the Eisenhower administration*. London: Macmillan.

Hurst, S. R. (2010). Next Obama test is Afghanistan. *Associated Press – Analysis*, April 3, 2010.

Hussein, Khalil Ibn (2007). 5 million Iraqi orphans, anti-corruption board reveals. *Aswat Al Iraq* (English language version), December 15, 2007

Johnson. H. (1964). *The bay of pigs*. London: Hutchinson.

Johnson, Lyndon B. (1958). My political philosophy. *The Texas Quarterly*, 1958.

Johnson, Lyndon B. (1968). Remarks on decision not to seek re-election, March 31, 1968. Charlottesville, VA: Miller Center of Public Affairs.

Johnson, Lyndon B. (1971). *The vantage point*. New York: Holt, Rinehart, & Winston.

Kaplan, Fred (2004). Ron and Mikhail's excellent adventure: How Reagan won the cold war. Posted Wednesday, June 9, 2004, at 7:29 PM ET on *Slate* (http://www.slate.com/id/2102081/).

Karnow, S. (1983). *Vietnam: A history*. New York: Viking.

Keating, J. (2009). IAEA demands to inspect Israeli nukes. *Foreign Policy, Passport Blog,* September 18, 2009.

Kennan, George F. (1958). *Russia, the atom, and the West*. London: Oxford University Press.

Kennedy, P. M. (1987). *The rise and fall of the great powers: Economic change and military conflict from 1500 to 2000*. New York: Random House.

Kessler, G. (2010). Clinton rebukes Israel over East Jerusalem plans, cites damage to bilateral ties. *Washington Post*, March 13, 2010.

Kiernan, B. (2002). *How Pol Pot came to power*. New Haven CT: Yale University Press.

Kiernan, B. (2004). *The Pol Pot regime*. New Haven CT: Yale University Press.

Kline, Joe (2008). The aimless war: Why are we in Afghanistan? *Time Magazine,* December 22, 2008.

Knebel, F. & Bailey, C. W. (1963). Secret revealed after 18 years: Fight in the United States over the A-bomb. *Look*, August 6, 1963.

Krock, T. J. (1992). *To end all wars: Woodrow Wilson and the quest for a new world order*. New York: Oxford University Press.

Landler, M., & Meyers, S. L. (2011). Obama sees '67 borders as starting point for peace deal. *New York Times*, 19 May, 2011.

Lehrer, Jim (2003). Sharing power. *NewsHour with Jim Lehrer*, September 15, 2003.

LoBaido, A. (2010). U.S. armed Pol Pot, say eyewitnesses. *WorldNetDaily*, March 26, 2010 (Google: A. LoBaido US armed Pol Pot).

Maley, W., & Saikal, A. (1989). *The Soviet withdrawal from Afghanistan*. Cambridge: Cambridge University Press.

Marston, J. (1997). *Cambodia 1991-94: Hierarchy, neutrality and etiquettes of discourse*. Seattle WA: University of Washington (doctoral dissertation).

Mazzetti, M., & Cooper, H. (2007). An Israeli strike on Syria kindles debate in the U.S. *New York Times*, October 10, 2007.

McCloy, John J.(1953). *The challenges to American foreign policy*. Cambridge, MA: Harvard University Press.

McNamara, R. S., Blight, J., Brigham, R. K., Biersteker, T. J., & Schandler, H. (2000). *Argument without end: In search of answers to the Vietnam tragedy*. New York: Public Affairs.

MHRI (2008). 4.5 millions orphans in Iraq. *Monitoring Net of Human Rights in Iraq,* January, 21, 2008.

Miles, H. (2007). Inconvenient truths. *London Review of Books,* June 21, 2007, pp. 8-10.

Milosz, C. (1953). *The captive mind.* New York: Knopf.

Morgenthau, Hans J. (1948). *Politics among nations.* New York: Knopf.

Morgenthau, Hans J. (1951). *In defense of the national interest.* New York: Knopf.

Morris, B. (20080. *1948: A History of the First Arab-Israeli War.* New Haven CN: Yale University Press.

Morton, Louis (1957). The decision to use the atomic bomb. *Foreign Affairs,* January, 1957.

Munton, A., & Welch, D. A. (2007). *The Cuban Missile Crisis: A Concise History.* New York: Oxford University Press

Nagy, Thomas (2001). The secret behind the sanctions: How the U.S. intentionally destroyed Iraq's water supply. *The Progressive,* September, 2001.

Neal, Fred Warner (1961). *U.S. foreign policy and the Soviet Union.* Santa Barbara, CAL: Center for the Study of Democratic Institutions.

NTI (2010). *Israel profile: Nuclear overview as of August 2010.* Washington DC: Nuclear Threat Initiative Library.

Nye, J. S. (2002). *The paradox of American power: Why the world's superpower can't go it alone.* New York: Oxford University Press.

Opotowsky, S. (1961). *The Kennedy government.* Edinburg: Harrap.

Oz, Amos (2003). *A tale of love and darkness.* New York: Harcourt.

Personal Security Board (1954). *Transcript of hearings before personal security board in the matter of Dr. J. Robert Oppenheimer, April 12 to May 6, 1954.* Washington, DC: Government Printing Office.

Phillips, D. L. (2004). Turkey's dreams of accession. *Foreign Affairs,* September/October 2004, vol. 83, pp. 86-97.

Peirce, G. (2009). The framing of al-Megrahi. *London Review of Books,* September 24, 2009, pp. 3-8.

PLO Mission to the United States (2009). Google "Israeli wall and settlements (July 2009)".

Quandt, W. B. (1993). *Peace process: American diplomacy and the Arab-Israeli conflict since 1967.* Berkeley: University of California Press. See p. 349 for Shamir.

Ridgeway, Matthew B., & Martin, H. H. (1956). *Soldier: Memoirs of Matthew B. Ridgeway.* New York: Harper.

Roberts, C. M. (1954). The day we didn't go to war. *Reporter,* September, 1954.

Rogin, Josh (2010). U.S. official: Obama's list for Netanyahu open to negotiation. *Foreign Policy – The Cable*, Thursday, April 1, 2010.

Roth, Joseph (1932). *The Radetzky March* (English edition: Trans. Edith Tucker & Geoffrey Dunlop. London: Allen Lane, 1974).

Rummel, R.J. (1997). *Statistics of democide: Genocide and mass murder since 1900*. Charlottesville VA: University of Virginia. Also, Piscataway NJ: Transaction Publishers.

Rusk, Dean (1966). Rusk's statement to House Panel on U.S. policy toward Communist China. *New York Times*, April 17, 1966.

Schlesinger, Arthur M. Jr. (1965). *A thousand days*. London: Andre Deutsch.

Shepard, Scott (2003). Bush: No Iraq link to 9/11 found. *Cox News Service*, 18 September1 2003 (www.seattlepi.com/national/140133_bushiraq18.html).

Sidey, Hugh (1964). *John F. Kennedy: A portrait*. London: Andre Deutsch.

Slocomb, M. (2004). *The People's Republic of Kampuchea, 1979-1989: The revolution after Pol Pot*. Seattle WA: University of Washington Press.

Sluglett, P. (2008). Imperial legacy: Lessons from British rule in Iraq? *History Compass*, June 28, 2008.

Smith, A. K. (1958). Behind the decision to use the atom bomb: Chicago 1944-45. *Bulletin of the Atomic Scientists*, October, 1958.

Sorensen. Theodore C. (1965). *Kennedy*. London: Hodder and Stoughton.

Sowell, Thomas (2003). Dangers ahead--from the right. *Capitalism magazine*, January 5, 2003.

Sowell Thomas (2009). *Intellectuals and society*. New York: Basic Books.

Spanier, John (1962). *American foreign policy since World War II* (revised ed.). New York: Praeger.

Stat. Sum. See *Statistical Summary: America's Major Wars, Table II (casualties)* at: www.cwc.other/stats/warcost.htm

Stimson, Henry L. (1947). The decision to use the atomic bomb. *Harper's*, February, 1947.

Stimson, Henry L., & Bundy, McGeorge (1948). *On active service in peace and war*. New York: Harper.

Sumner, William Graham (1899). The conquest of the United States by Spain. Speech to the Phi Beta Kappa Society of Yale University, January 16, 1899.

Szulc, T., & Meyer, K. E. (1962). *The Cuban invasion*. New York: Ballantine.

Talbott, S. (1989). America abroad: Defanging the beast. *Time*, February 6, 1989.

Tang Tsou (1963). *America's failure in China, 1941-1950*. Chicago: University of Chicago Press.

Tessler, M. (1994). *A history of the Israeli-Palestinian conflict*. Bloomington: University of Indiana Press. See p. 207 for Begin.

Truman, Harry S. (1955). *Year of decisions*. Garden City NY: Doubleday.

Tucker, S. C. (1999). *Vietnam*. Lexington KY: University Press of Kentucky.

Tucker, S. C., ed. (2000). *Encyclopedia of the Vietnam war: A political, social, and military history*. New York: Oxford University Press.

UNAMA (2010). *United Nations Human Rights Office report on Afghanistan*. United Nations Assistance Mission in Afghanistan, 31 March 2010.

UNICEF (1999). *Results of the 1999 Iraq child and maternal mortality surveys*. New York: UNICEF Publications,

US Army (2005). The U. S. Army in Vietnam from Tet to the final withdrawal. In R. W. Stewart (ed.), *American military history, Vol. II, The United States Army in a global era, 1917-2003*. Washington DC: US Army Center of Military History.

US Department of Defense (1969). *United States-Vietnam Relations: 1945-1967, Vol. 1, The air war in North Vietnam*. Washington DC: Department of Defense.

US News and World Report (1963). See issue September 9, 1963.

Vandenbroucke, L. S. (1984). The Israeli Strike against OSIRAQ: The dynamics of fear and proliferation in the Middle East. *Air University Review*, September-October 1984.

Vickery, M. (1984). *Cambodia: 1975-1982*. Boston: South End Press.

Vogelsang, W. (2002). *The Afghans*. Oxford UK: Blackwell Publishers.

Wallensteen, P., Staibano, C., & Eriksson,M. (2003). *Making targeted sanctions effective*. Uppsala, Sweden: Department of Peace and Conflict Research.

Weiss, S., & Dougan, C. (1983). *Nineteen sixty-eight: Vietnam experience*. Newton, MA: Boston Publishing Company.

Welch, Matt (2002). The politics of dead children: Have sanctions against Iraq murdered millions? *Reason Magazine*, March 2002.

Wikipedia (2010). Google 'Vietnam war—loss of life by year'.

Wise, D., & Ross, T. B. (1964). *The invisible government*. New York: Random House.

Yakovlev, Aleksandr (1992). Quoted in *The New Yorker*, November 2, 1992.

Zhai, Qiang (2000). *China and the Vietnam Wars, 1950–1975*. Chapel Hill NC: University of North Carolina Press.

# *Index*

*Beyond Patriotism*